Guidance, Supplement to THE SPIRIT LED™ Life

IN THE WHOLE COUNSEL OF GOD

Wayne Kim

CCAH PRESS

Acknowledgments

Our Lord is glorified forever. The Bible Study groups at A242, Fountain, Rock, Sunrise, Telacu, and on-line course are thanked for asking deep questions out of their spiritually led lives. Kevin and Philip are thanked for their designing this book. Gerson and Joseph also are thanked for their editing. The abundant spiritual fruits to each member at CCAH or every believer on the earth may be produced by our God, out of his daily intimate fellowship with our Lord in the fullness of the Spirit, according to every word of God which he might understand with this book as a mere reference book. New grooms and brides, both Alex & Joyce and Daniel & Heather, are congratulated on wedding in July, 2011, and this book is dedicated to them as well as to the life time staff members – Christian, George, Henry, Jeremy, Joseph, Lucas, Reza, and Seoung -- and the faithful stewards – Bernice, Christine, Dave, Doreene, Margaret, and Pam. Finally, Alex, Carl, Chuck, Gerson, and Lily are thanked for their continual prayer supports & labors. Our Lord is thanked for these things and in everything.

Wayne Kim

CONTENTS

Cover Back Page	5
Testimonial Preface	13
I. The Christian	21
II. To the World	23
A. Witness	23
B. Preaching	26
III. The Knowledge of God	28
A. Every Thought	29
B. Why Only the Bible?	88
1. Faith Statement	96
2. Whole Counsel of God	102
IV. The Lord's Prayer	111
V. Personal Questions	113
Appendix 2	115

Calvary Chapel Anaheim Hills (CCAH) Press
PO Box 27693
Anaheim Hills, CA 92809

All quotations, except the King James Version of the Bible (KJV), are taken from the New King James Version, © 1982 by Thomas Nelson, Inc. Used by permission. All rights reserved.

Guidance, Q & A, or Supplement to The Spirit Led ™ *Life in the Whole Counsel of God* provides a depth, arising out of the Bible study groups' questions in their lives, to make our lives to be led by the Spirit according to the Word of God -- per each chapter on The Spirit Led ™ Life book, by giving some guidance, by answering each question, or by giving some supplements. Q & A stands for Questions & Answers. The questions' page numbers ("p") on *The Spirit Led* ™ *Life in the Whole Counsel of God* book are parenthesized as a reference for the entire Bible study. Emphasized words are underlined or boldfaced. The plain and simple words & charts are used for the general public who might understand, avoiding difficulty.

ISBN 9780984431823
© Copyright 2011 by Wayne Kim. All rights reserved. No part of this book may be reproduced in any forms or by any means without the prior written permission of the publisher, except for brief quotations in critical articles or reviews.

Library of Congress Control Number: 2011905543
Printed in the United States of America

Cover Back Page

Guidance

To overview, we can answer briefly the self questions to confront excerpted from the book of *The Spirit Led* ™ *Life in the Whole Counsel of God.*

Q & A

"What's difference between the Spirit led life and the Self led life?" (p 27)

The Spirit led life is the life which is led by the Holy Spirit, while the Self led life is the life which is led by the Self.

"What's difference between the spiritual discernment & the carnal judgment?" (p 46)

The spiritual discernment is to discern thoughts at the standard of the Bible in the Spirit, while the carnal judgment is to judge them out of carnality/flesh such as critic, hatred, jealousy, or arrogance.

"What is a guideline for preaching?" (p 44)

It is a parable, a sin problem, resolution, response, and prayer.

"How can I preach to people if I am busy to work?" (p 44)

We can simply place gospel tracts for salvation on a proper place, to be picked up by people.

"Can the Holy Spirit work against the Bible?" (p 31)

No. The Holy Spirit is one of three persons in one God. The Holy Spirit is God. So, The Holy Spirit can't work against the Word of God, i.e., God can't work against His own word, but the Holy Spirit is teaching all things God said (John 14:26).

"What's difference between Christianity and Religion?" (p 31)

Christianity is from God to a man, while Religion is from a man to a god.

"What are potential dangers of having the gift of miracles?" (p 75)

The dangers are to use the gift for his personal benefit and to take his own glory rather than to acknowledge God's glory.

"Is every human thought more important than the knowledge of God?" (p 74)

No, it is not more important than the knowledge of God but we can use it as a mere tool to understand His knowledge faithfully.

"How do I know God's direction?" (p 123)

To know His direction, we often should consider 3 factors – (1) 100 % God's glory; (2) applicable verses in the Bible; and (3) open circumstances.

"What is the real issue of church governments?" (p 75)

It is whether or not decision makers are equipped with the Whole Counsel of God in the work of the Holy Spirit, i.e., whether the church is governed by God.

"Is my life changed upon the faith of Jesus' 2nd coming soon? How is it changed?" (p 94)

Upon the faith of Jesus' 2nd coming soon, our life is changed as (1) we can be raptured during our life; (2) we can have a constant exceeding hope to meet our Lord soon, joyfully; (3) we are constrained with AGAPE love to preach to unbelievers more and more before His urgent coming; (4) The priority of our life is always the kingdom of God or eternal thing over temporary or earthly thing; (5) we are purified or sanctified to the image of Christ who is coming soon.

"What does TULIP stand for?" (p 101)

The thought of John Calvin is described with the five (5) points – Total Depravity (T), Unconditional Election (U), Limited Atonement (L), Irresistible Grace (I), and Perseverance of the Saints (P).

"Is my faith the concurrent condition for election?" (p 102)

Yes. Faith is the concurrent condition of regeneration because upon my faith, not after faith, regeneration starts at the same time as faith.

"What destroy my ministry to the Lord?" (p 140)

An ivy tower, institutionalization, and 3 G (abbreviated girl, gold, and girl terms) destroy the ministry to the Lord, not out of the work of the Spirit.

"What is Prosperity Gospel?" (p 162)

It is the Gospel that God provides His children material prosperity, wealth, and physical health.

"What is Evolutional Creation?" (P 162)

God uses evolution process as a tool of God's creation.

"What is Witness Lee?" (p 162)

Witness Lee established Living Stream Ministry (LSM), promoting Watchman Nee - imprisoned in 1952 for his faith and dead in 1972 - who wrote "The Normal Christian Life," with the strong opposition of denominational churches.

"What is Emerging Church?" (p 162)

Emerging or Emergent Church appears a church who seeks to deconstruct the meaning of the Bible and to reconstruct the meaning combined with thoughts of people who live in a postmodern culture or postmodernism.

"Can I see my neighbor who doesn't believe in Christ? What is his thought? Can I get a parable or an opening statement to deliver Gospel from these thoughts?" (p 162)

If we can see an unbeliever neighbor, we can develop a parable close to our neighbor's thought without offense in the Spirit from the cast down thoughts from pages 148 through 161.

"Are human proofs sufficient to prove "Absolute truth" of the Bible?" (p 170)

No, any human proofs are not sufficient to prove "Absolute truth" of the Bible because we can't understand the absolute truth of the Bible unless the Holy Spirit given by infinite God reveals His wisdom to us.

"What's difference between the gifts & the fruit of the Spirit?" (p 190)

The gifts of the Spirit are given by the Spirit in 1 Corinthians 12:8-10 & Romans 12:5-8 (e.g. wisdom, knowledge, discerning of spirits, faith, healings, miracles, prophecy, tongues, interpretation of tongues, ministry, teaching, exhortation, giving with liberality, leading with diligence, and mercy with cheerfulness), while the fruit of the Spirit is Agape love described as several attributes in Galatians 5:22-23 (8 terms – joy, peace, long suffering, kindness, goodness, faithfulness, gentleness, and self-control) and 1 Corinthians 13:4-8 (e.g. suffers long, kind, etc.)

"Can I put God into a man-made-frame?" (p 101)

No, because all men as creatures come short of God's glory (Romans 3:23). Overemphasizing portions can fall into a man-made-frame different from all the Scripture given by inspiration of God.

"Is God's truth dependent upon my wisdom or defense?" (p 169)

No, because God's truth is perfect, infallible, inerrant, authoritative or absolute, being independent upon our wisdom or defense. But our wisdom merely might be helpful for us to understand His truth.

"What's a guideline for the Bible study?" (p 200)

A guideline is suggested for the Bible study of a prayer, observation, interpretation, application, and a prayer.

"What is a big picture for the Lord's prayer?" (p 204)

Two parts in a big picture are Worship and Petition.

"What is my compelling motive to minister?"(p 212)

Love of Christ should be my compelling motive to minister to the Lord and His sheep.

"Am I fruitful for the kingdom of God?"(p 212)

I should examine by myself whether or not Agape love overflows in my life because Agape love is the genuine evidence of the Holy Spirit.

Supplement

In the back title of "**The Whole Counsel of God**" in Acts 20:27(NKJV) is translated as "all the counsel of God" in KJV and "the whole will of God" in New International Version (NIV). There are a lot of English versions of the Bible.

Issue is **which version we should use,** i.e., which version is close to the original Bible (the Hebrew in the Old Testament; the Greek in the New Testament). We'd like to avoid a tedious argument, which one is better between KJV translated from Textus Receptus and NIV translated from Alexandrian Text.

In light of 2 Timothy 3:16," All Scripture *is* given by inspiration of God, and *is* profitable for doctrine, for reproof, for correction, for instruction in righteousness," Deuteronomy 4:2, "You shall not add to the word which I command you, nor take from it, that you may keep the commandments of the LORD your God which I command you," and Matthew 28:20, "teaching them to observe <u>all things</u> that I have commanded you; and lo, I am with you always, *even* to the end of the age." Amen," we'd like to use KJV or NKJV as the textbook of "the whole counsel of God" but NIV or any other versions as reference books. Although NIV is the most popular, we don't adopt it as the textbook because in NIV Matthew 17:21, 18:11, 23:14, and Mark 11:26, 15:28, and Luke 17:36, 23:17 are not found.

Testimonial Preface

(P 8-24)

Guidance

Everybody has his personal biographical testimony, but the testimony is different between a believer and an unbeliever. The believer states how God has worked in his life, while the unbeliever states how he has lived his life.

The believer is baptized by immersion or sprinkling.

Supplement

In light of Deuteronomy 6, God says in verse 17, "You shall diligently keep the commandments of the LORD your God, His testimonies, and His statutes which He has commanded you," and in verses 20 and 21, "When your son asks you in time to come, saying, 'What *is the meaning of* the testimonies, the statutes, and the judgments which the LORD our God has commanded you?' [21] then you shall say to your son: 'We were slaves of Pharaoh in Egypt, and the LORD brought us out of Egypt with a mighty hand," our testimonies should be His testimonies to glorify Him always, not to glorify ourselves. For even our disadvantages in our life the Lord can be thanked unless the disadvantages are caused by our sins, because in us the works of God should be revealed as Jesus said in John 9:2-3, "And His disciples asked Him, saying, "Rabbi, who sinned, this man or his parents, that he was born blind?" [3] Jesus answered,

"Neither this man nor his parents sinned, but that the works of God should be revealed in him."

Even if Paul persecuted Christians during his life, Paul testified that God separated him from his mother's womb, and called him by His grace (Galatians 1:15), **acknowledging how God has worked in his life** for His sake.

Paul's Biography

Years	Bible	Area	Event
35 AD	Acts 9:4-6	Damascus	Persecution of Christians; Paul's conversion
for 3 years	Galatians 1:17; Acts 9:21-26 (3 years gap)	Desert of Arabia / Damascus	Divine Revelation "Gospel of Grace"
38 AD	Galatians 1:19; Acts 9:26-27	Jerusalem	1st visit; met only James
for 7 years	Galatians 1:21; Acts 9:30 "Tarsus"	Syria(Antioch) &Cilicia(Tarsus)	Stayed in Tarsus
45 AD	Acts 11:25 "Barnabas went to Tarsus to seek Saul"	Antioch	Started ministry in his home church. 10 years preparation.

49 AD (Probably 14 years after conversion)	Galatians 2:1-10 (Acts 11:29-30? Acts 15:2?)	Jerusalem/ other areas	Other visits
52 AD	Acts 18:22 "Antioch"		
57 AD	Acts 21:5 "Tyre"		

Further, Paul gave **thanks to the Lord for his thorn in his flesh** in 2 Corinthians 12:7-10, "And lest I should be exalted above measure by the abundance of the revelations, a thorn in the flesh was given to me, a messenger of Satan to buffet me, lest I be exalted above measure. [8] Concerning this thing I pleaded with the Lord three times that it might depart from me. [9] And He said to me, "My grace is sufficient for you, for My strength is made perfect in weakness." Therefore most gladly I will rather boast in my infirmities, that the power of Christ may rest upon me. [10] Therefore I take pleasure in infirmities, in reproaches, in needs, in persecutions, in distresses, for Christ's sake. For when I am weak, then I am strong." Likewise, I have also thanked to the Lord for stutter symptom (like a thorn in my flesh). I prefer writing to talking to overcome it for Christ's sake. Before talking (e.g. teaching), I often prepare for its writing.

When we believe in Jesus Christ as our Lord and savior, we have an **ordinance of water baptism** (p 8). God says in Romans 6: 4-5, "Therefore we were buried with Him through baptism into death, that just as Christ was raised from the dead by the glory of the Father, even so we also should walk in newness of life.[5] For if we have been united

<u>together</u> in the likeness of His death, certainly we also shall be *in the likeness* of *His* resurrection." Since the water represents the grave, when we immerge into water, our old lives after the flesh are dead to sin, symbolized with Christ' death on cross. While we come out of the water, we have new lives after the Spirit to God, symbolized with Christ's resurrection. Our master is no longer sin or Satan, whom Adam obeyed to, but God through our faith in Christ. We as believers are free to choose between God and sin, i.e., the Holy Spirit and the flesh (the body contaminated with Adam's original sin) in Romans 8:1, "T*here is* therefore now no condemnation to those who are in Christ Jesus, who do not walk according to the flesh, but according to the Spirit." Sprinkling water on head is not originated from the Bible but from church history because baptism (BAPTIZO the Greek in the Bible) means originally "immersion," neither "sprinkling" (RANTIZO the Greek) nor "pouring"(CHEO the Greek), The baptism by sprinkling or pouring substituted for the baptism by immersion is practiced for the symbol of Christ's death & resurrection in some denominations.

Christ's death & resurrection (p 14-15) is stated in four (4) Gospels as historically occurred. In our calendar day, we can see the historical occurrence between often called Palm Sunday and Easter Sunday as the following time table; but neither Jewish calendar nor Roman calendar is specified in the Gospels. So we could reasonably infer days and times in order to understand the events stated in the Gospels :

This view of the time table is one view in light of Synoptic Gospels (Matthew, Mark, and Luke) adopting the Jewish calendar and the Gospel of John adopting the Roman calendar (the origin of our calendar). The

Jewish time is 6 hours in advance from the Roman time and a Jewish day begins at evening or sunset (Genesis 1:5), and so the Passover begins at evening (Exodus 12:6; Leviticus 23:5). The Lord's Supper often called as the "Last Supper" or "communion" took place close to the Passover in light of "before the feast of the Passover" in John 13:1 and "ready the Passover" in Matthew 26:19 & in Mark 14:16, that is, close to the Thursday evening in our calendar. Jesus said in Matthew 12:40, "For as Jonah was three days and three nights in the belly of the great fish, so will the Son of Man be three days and three nights in the heart of the earth." In one view of the Roman calendar, a new day begins at midnight and ends at midnight of the next day, sufficing "3 days" with Friday, Saturday, and Sunday and "3 nights" with Friday sunset to midnight, Saturday night before sunrise and Saturday sunset to midnight, and Sunday night before sunrise.

In another view of the Jewish calendar in all four Gospels, a new day begins at evening or sunset and ends at evening or sunset of the next day. It is viewed that Jesus was crucified on the Thursday evening in our calendar (then, Friday began in the Jewish calendar) with the double Sabbaths, sufficing "3 days and 3 nights" and rose again "in the end of the Sabbath, as it began to dawn toward the first day of the week (Matthew 28:1)," that is, Sunday sunrise in both Jewish calendar and our calendar. This view would cause to change like italicized one of the time table. Also, if a different view comes again unless the view is contrary to the word of God in the Bible (e.g. 1 Corinthians 11:23, "on the *same* night in which He was betrayed took bread"), the view would cause to change the time table too. **The various, different, or inconsistent times** discovered or alleged by archeologists show the insufficiency of human thoughts, compared with the sufficiency of His word. However, further discoveries may make clear up some inconsistent times.

Therefore, this time table is a mere reference for us to understand the events stated in the Gospels faithfully. The understanding might develop our relationship with Christ closer. So, the times and days in the time table are not a substance but the substance is "Christ's death & resurrection" events stated in the Gospels (here, cross-references in the Gospels) for us in light of Colossians 2:16-17, "So let no one judge you in food or in drink, or regarding a festival or a new moon or Sabbaths, [17] which are a shadow of things to come, but the substance is of Christ."

Christ(C)'s Death & Resurrection (*Our vs *Jewish calendar*)

Sun	Mon	Tue	Wed	Thu	Fri	Sun
MORNING Triumphal Entry in Jerusalem	Cleaning Temple	1.Question of C's Authority 2. Widow's two mites offering	Woman's anointing C at Bethany	1. Washing feet of 12 disciples 2. Last Supper; 3.Prayer in Gethsemane	Sanhedrin + Pilate + Herod + Pilate **C's crucifixion (9 AM) Noon (Darkness) About 3 PM (Passed away) J's Burial	*** Res urre ctio n [Eas ter]
EVENING						
Mon	*Tue*	*Wed*	*Thu*	*Fri*	*Sat*	*Mon*

			Judah's betrayal in heart	C's arrest C's trial (Annas + Caiphas + Peter's denial)	*(+ 1 day: Double Sabbaths)*		
CROSS-REFERENCES Mt 21:1-11 Lk 19:28-40	Mt 21:12-17 Lk 19:45-48	Lk 20:1-8 Mt 21:23-27 Lk 21:1-4	Mk14:3-9 Jn 12:4-6 Mk 14:10-11 Lk 22:1-6 Mt 26:14-16 Jn 13:1-2	Jn 13:3-30 Lk 22:7-23 Mk 14:12-26 Mt 26:26-30 Lk 22: 39-45 Mk 14:27-42 Mt 26:36-46 Lk 22: 47-71 Mt 26:47-75 Mk 14:43-72	Lk22:66-71 Lk 23:1-7 Lk 23:8-25 Mt 27 Mk 15:25 Lk 23:50-56 Jn 19	Lk 24:1 Mt 28:1
Sun	Mon	Tue	Wed	Thu	Fri		Sun

* A Jewish day begins at evening;
Jewish time => Our time: ("this 3rd hour"
Mark 15:25 => 9 AM; "the 9th hour"
Matthew 27:46 => 3 PM)

** 7 statements on the cross
   (1) Luke 23:34
   (2) Luke 23:43
   (3) John 19:26-27

* ** Resurrection
1. Time Table "3 (+40) 43 (+7) 50"
(1) Passover (Crucifixion)
(2) 3 days (Burial + Resurrection)
(3) 40 days (Resurrected C's teaching on earth; Acts 1:3; C's ascension, Acts 1:9)
(4) Pentecost (50 days as of the Passover; 7 days after C's

(4) Matthew 27:46 (5) John 19:28 (6) John 19:30 (7) Luke 23:46	ascension[1]) The Spirit came 2. Eye Witnesses (1) Luke 24:10; Matthew 28:9 (2) Luke 24:34-35 (3) John 20:27 (4) Mark 16:14 (5) 1 Corinthians 15:5-8

---

[1] See http://www.churchyear.net/pentecost.html - Different time "10 days after Christ's ascension"

I. The Christian

(P 25-27)

Guidance

The definition of the Christian stated in the Bible over abused Christian term is discussed: What is a Christian? A missionary's testimony shows that to claim a Christian is not enough, according to the Word of God.

Q & A

(1) Am I the Christian stated in the Bible? Do I love anything or anyone more than Jesus? If so, how should I do?

As long as we are the believers only in Jesus Christ as our Lord and Savior, each of us is the Christian stated in the Bible. If we love anything more than Jesus, Jesus is no longer our Lord, so that we should repent it and petition God to forgive it in the name of our Lord Jesus Christ.

(2) What's difference between the Spirit led life and the Self led life?

The Spirit led life is the life which is led by the Holy Spirit, while the Self led life is the life which is led by the Self.

Supplement

We are singing the new song of "Most of All[2]" from our hearts to praise our Lord with Chaster, Doreene, Evelene, Maria, Kay, etc:

> "Jesus I love You most of all
> Most of all I love You
> Jesus I love You most of all
> Most of all I love You
>
> You are my God, my best friend
> I'm stickin' with You Lord till the end
> Jesus I want the world to know
> That I love You most of all
> (*Repeat*)
>
> Jesus I love You most of all
> Most of all I love You
> Jesus I love You most of all
> Most of all I love You"

We should do so for our daily lives. Christians are often called in the Bible as believers, brothers, saints or the righteous, while non-Christians as unbelievers, natural men, or the unrighteous (e.g. 1 Corinthians 6:1,6).

---

[2] Chuck Smith, et al, "Most of All" (California: Calvary Chapel Music, 2003).

II. To the World

A. Witness

(P 28-32)

Guidance

How Christians should be witnesses to Christ in the World is discussed. We will become witnesses to Jesus when the Holy Spirit comes upon us.

Q & A

(1) Can the Holy Spirit work against the Bible?

No. The Holy Spirit is one of three persons in one God. The Holy Spirit is God. So, the Holy Spirit can't work against the Word of God, i.e., God can't work against His own word but the Holy Spirit is teaching all things God said (John 14:26).

(2) What's difference between Christianity and Religion?

Christianity is from God to a man, while Religion is from a man to a god.

(3) How can I become a witness to Christ?

When the Holy Spirit comes upon us, i.e., Baptism with the Holy Spirit, we shall be witnesses to Christ anywhere.

(4) What are Christ's great commandments?

Christ's great commandments are to love God with all our heart, soul, mind, and strength and to love our neighbors as ourselves.

Supplement

Who is our neighbor? (p 30)

After Jesus taught the Great commandments, a certain lawyer asked the same question as our Bible Study Group's member. And Jesus answered in Luke 10:29-37 "But he, wanting to justify himself, said to Jesus, "And <u>who is my neighbor</u>?" [30] Then Jesus answered and said: "A certain *man* went down from Jerusalem to Jericho, and fell among thieves, who stripped him of his clothing, wounded *him,* and departed, leaving *him* half dead. [31] Now by chance a certain priest came down that road. And when he saw him, he passed by on the other side. [32] Likewise a Levite, when he arrived at the place, came and looked, and passed by on the other side. [33] But a certain Samaritan, as he journeyed, came where he was. And when he saw him, he had <u>compassion</u>. [34] So he went to *him* and <u>bandaged</u> his wounds, pouring on <u>oil and wine</u>; and he set him on his own animal, brought him to an inn, and <u>took care of</u> him. [35] On the next day, when he departed, he took out two denarii, gave *them* to the innkeeper, and said to him, 'Take care of him; and whatever more you spend, when I come again, I will repay you.' [36] So which of these three do you think was neighbor to him who fell among the thieves?" [37] And he said, "He who showed mercy on him." Then Jesus said to him, "Go and do likewise." "   It is exposed that a neighbor is one of them in near relationship, here, between the Samaritan and the victim of the thieves.

How can I love my neighbor as myself?

Our God gave us our physical life, the Holy Spirit, our spiritual life, free will, talents, and any other possessions. Like the Samaritan with the things given by God, we may have compassion upon our neighbor, followed by several consequences like giving away own materials (oil & wine), skills (bandage), labor/time (take care of), or money (two denarii). This practice to love our neighbor as ourselves might give an opportunity to him for his salvation which is the eternal value incomparable to any values on earth.

B. Preaching

(P 33-44)

Guidance

In Matthew 9:35, "Then Jesus went about <u>all</u> the cities and villages, <u>teaching</u> in their synagogues, <u>preaching</u> the gospel of the kingdom, and <u>healing</u> every sickness and every disease among the people," Christ's main ministries on the earth were three – teaching, preaching, and healing. One of three is the preaching toward unbelievers. How we should do preaching to the World is guided.

Q & A

(1) What's the goal of my preaching?

The goal of our preaching is to plant the seed of salvation to unbelievers or to introduce Gospel to unbelievers for their salvation.

(2) What is a guideline for preaching? Do I use it today?

A guideline for preaching is a parable, a sin problem, resolution, response, and prayer. As long as we have a heart to love the soul of an unbeliever, we can use it today in preaching.

(3) How can I preach to people if I am busy to work?

We can simply place gospel tracts for salvation on a proper place, to be picked up by people.

Supplement

In the Romans 11:12 (p 35), "For there is no different between Jew and Greek, for the same Lord over all is rich to all who call upon Him," the **favoritism or exclusion or discrimination** because of race or paternity is discouraged. However, a qualified minister[3] may be ordained by God even if he has either a same race or paternity relationship with his decision maker(s). For example, a pastor may succeed his father as senior pastor because of biblical qualification, not of paternity (Leviticus 10:1 and 6 "Aaron's sons to become priests"). Also, the believers who speak same language may meet together to understand the word of God even if all of them are same races, but they should not exclude a different racial believer who understands the language and wants to join there.

What do you mean "in season and out of season" in 2 Timothy 4:2? (p 44)

No mater what we think our time to preach is proper, preach the word anytime!

---

[3] A reference of "a qualified minister" may be "Ministerial Relations," on pages 223 through 226, at the appendix Bylaws.

III. The Knowledge of God

(P 45-46)

Guidance

How every human thought should be discerned to be accepted or cast down according to the Knowledge of God is guided, without a carnal judgment.

Q & A

What's difference between the spiritual discernment and the carnal judgment?

The spiritual discernment is to discern thoughts at the standard of the Bible in the Spirit, while the carnal judgment is to judge them out of carnality or flesh such as critic, hatred, jealousy, or arrogance.

Supplement

Judgment (p 46) is sometimes asked to us in the Bible, but that means the judgment controlled by the Spirit (not carnal judgment), which is a synonym of the spiritual discernment (e.g. 1 Corinthians 6:2 & 14:29). The "synonym" is understood in 1 Kings 3:9, "Therefore give to <u>Your servant</u> an understanding heart to <u>judge</u> Your people, that I may <u>discern between good and evil</u>. For who is able to judge this great people of Yours?"

A. Every Thought

(P 47-76)

Guidance

Every thought should be into captivity to the obedience of Christ (2 Corinthians 10:5). Obedient thought is encouraged, while framing thought is discouraged. When we read the Bible, our heart to obey is what God says to us, called as "obedient thoughts." However, to frame God's word into our thought is called as "framing thought."

Supplement

Although sometimes we don't understand God's word, **we should wait for Him to reveal it** because God says in both John 21:25, "And there are also many other things that Jesus did, which if they were written one by one, I suppose that even the world itself could not contain the books that would be written. Amen," and 2 Peter 3:16, "as also in all his epistles, speaking in them of these things, in which are some things hard to understand, which untaught and unstable *people* twist to their own destruction, as *they do* also the rest of the Scriptures."

(1) Living Water

Guidance

Living water, the Holy Spirit's identity, His work, His gifts, our response to Him, and so on are discussed. Living Water is a symbol of the Holy Spirit in John 7:38-39, "He who believes in Me, as the Scripture has said, out of his heart will flow rivers of <u>living water</u>." [39] But this He spoke <u>concerning the Spirit</u>, whom those believing in Him would receive; for the Holy Spirit was not yet *given,* because Jesus was not yet glorified."

Q & A

(1) Is every human thought more important than the knowledge of God?

No, it is not more important than the knowledge of God but we can use it as a mere tool to understand His knowledge faithfully.

(2) Who is conforming me into the image of Jesus Christ?

The Holy Spirit is to conform us into the image of Jesus Christ.

(3) Under whose direction, can I preach Christ?

Under the direction of the Holy Spirit, we can preach Christ. For example, under the direction of the Holy Spirit, Peter preached Christ to Cornelius and his friends (Acts 11:1-10).

(4) What's the purpose of my prayer?

The purpose of our prayer is that we open our hearts to allow God to do the things He wants to do.

(5) What does the word of "differences of ministries" mean?

The word of "differences of ministries" in 1 Corinthians 12:5, "There are differences of ministries, but the same Lord," means that the same Lord directs all different ministries of – apostle, prophet, pastor-teacher, government, helps, etc.

(6) Why is my knowledge without wisdom dangerous?

The knowledge without wisdom is dangerous because through such knowledge we have been able to create super weapons with the capacity to destroy mankind.

(7) How does the lack of the gift of wisdom often lead in the Church?

The lack of the gift of wisdom often leads division within the Church.

(8) What are three kinds of faith?

The three kinds of faith are described in the Bible: (1) <u>Saving faith</u> is trusting in the Lord Jesus Christ as our Savior, believing that He paid the price for our sins; (2) Our trust in the promises of God is the kind of faith growing as we experience the faithfulness of God, as called as <u>Growing Faith</u>; and (3) <u>Healing faith</u> is the gift of faith from our close relationship with the Spirit,

(9) What are potential dangers of having the gift of miracles?

The dangers are to use the gift for his personal benefit and to take his own glory rather than to acknowledge God's glory.

(10) How can I judge the prophecy in the Spirit?

The three scriptural bases for the judging prophecy are: whether or not (1) the prophecy lives with the already revealed Word of God (conflict); (2) it lines up with the fact; and (3) it honors Jesus Christ.

(11) What is the gift of tongue?

The gift of tongue is to speak fluently in an unknown language only to God through the agency of the Holy Spirit (1 Corinthians 14:2).

(12) What do "interpretation" and "minister" mean?

Interpretation means explanation of concepts. Minister never means profession, spiritual dictator, or coercive leader, but means servant or under rower.

(13) What is the purpose of the "pastor-teacher?"

The purpose of the "pastor-teacher" is to equip the believers to minister and to edify the body of Christ till we all come in the unity of the faith and of the knowledge of the Son of God, to be perfect.

(14) What is the baptism with the Holy Spirit?

The baptism with the Holy Spirit occurs when the Holy Spirit begins to overflow from us or to come upon (EPI) us (Acts 1:8).

(15) As gravity is a physical law, what is a spiritual law?

The Spiritual law is the law of giving.

(16) What's difference between justice and mercy?

Justice is exactly what we deserved but mercy is what we don't deserve.

(17) Do I have the genuine evidence of the Holy Spirit in my life?

To know that we have the evidence, we should examine ourselves in our lives whether or not His genuine evidence is Agape love and should prove ourselves.

(18) What's difference between regeneration experience and baptism with the Holy Spirit?

The difference between regeneration experience and baptism with the Holy Spirit is described as that experience is conversion, that is, indwelling the Holy Spirit, and this occurs separately subsequently overflowing the Holy Spirit.

(19) What does the Spirit lead me to do?

The Holy Spirit by Himself is God's gift. The Holy Spirit enables us to overcome sin, makes us to be conformed to the image of Jesus Christ, transforms us into a powerful witness for the Lord, and allows us to have the power to live for Jesus. When we ask for the fit of the Holy Spirit, by faith of God's promise, He leads us both to will and to do for His good pleasure (Philippians 2:13) such various areas as our hands to touch the needy, the afflicted, the sick or the suffering people; our voice to share His love and His truth; our heart to love all the people around us.

(20) What is the real issue of church governments?

The real issue is whether or not decision makers are equipped with the Whole Counsel of God in the work of the Holy Spirit, i.e., whether the church is governed by God.

Supplement

The Holy Spirit (p 48) is also stated in the Bible as the Spirit of God (Genesis 1:2), the Spirit of truth (John 16:13), the Spirit (Acts 18:5), the Spirit of holiness (Romans 1:4), the Spirit of Christ (Romans 8:29), or His Spirit (Romans 8:11), in some aspects.

Spiritual Gifts (p 55) in 1 Corinthians 12: 8-10, nine (9) things, can be divided into 3 sections, i.e., power (wisdom, knowledge, discerning of spirits), faith (faith, healings, miracles), utterance (prophecy, tongues, interpretation of tongues). Also, the seven (7) things of Spiritual Gifts are stated in Romans 12:5-8, "so we, *being* many, are one body in Christ, and individually members of one another. [6] Having then gifts differing according to the grace that is given to us, *let us use them:* if prophecy, *let us* (1) prophesy in proportion to our faith; [7] or ministry, *let us use it* in *our* (2) ministering; he who teaches, in (3) teaching; [8] he who exhorts, in (4) exhortation; he who (5) gives, with liberality; he who (6) leads, with diligence; he who shows (7) mercy, with cheerfulness." Please note the Spirit Himself is a gift of God upon our faith in Christ.

In **wisdom gift** (p 56), abortion, suicide, divorce, gambling, drug addiction, or alcoholism issue is raised. Those are generally discouraged according to the Bible. But those are not unpardonable sins (Matthew 12:32) because whoever commits abortion, attempted suicide, divorce, gambling, drug addiction, or alcoholism can be forgiven upon his repenting prayers to the Lord. (1) **Abortion** - Since a fetus in the belly is a person created in His image, abortion is discouraged in light of Jeremiah 1:5, ""Before I formed you in the womb I knew you; Before you were born I sanctified you; I ordained you a prophet to the nations." But, a purely raped conceived woman and/or a woman to deliver a baby at the risk of her life should be followed by her fervent prayer for the Lord's direction in purity. (2) **Suicide** – Since our body is the temple of the Holy Spirit, we shouldn't destroy our bodies by ourselves in light of 1 Corinthian 6:19-20, "Or do you not know that your body is the temple of the Holy Spirit *who is* in you, whom you have from God, and you are not your own? [20] For you were bought at a price; therefore glorify God in your body and in your spirit, which are God's." To a dead person who committed a suicide, nobody knows why he did so, not subject to third person's judgment. Further, his bereaved family members need comforts coming from God. (3) **Divorce** – Since marriage has been ordained by God, divorce should be discouraged in Matthew 19:5-6, "and said, *'For this reason a man shall leave his father and mother and be joined to his wife, and the two shall become one flesh'*? [6] So then, they are no longer two but one flesh. Therefore what God has joined together, let not man separate." Further, it is discussed below in the section of Marriage (Wedding). (4) **Gambling** – Since we should eat with our work, not with other's loss, gambling is discouraged in light 2 Thessalonians 3:12, "Now those who are such we command and exhort through our Lord Jesus Christ that they work in quietness and eat their own bread," and 1 Thessalonians 5:22, "Abstain from every form of evil," (e.g. state Lotto) and 1 Timothy 6:10, "For the love of money is a root of all *kinds of* evil, for which some have strayed from the faith in their greediness, and pierced themselves through with many sorrows." How about **investments** (e.g. stock, mutual fund, saving accounts, or real estates)? In Matthew 25:27, "So you ought to have deposited my money with the bankers, and at my coming I would have received back my own with interest," and in Ecclesiastes 11:1-2, "Cast your bread upon the waters, For you will find it after many days. ² Give a serving to seven, and also to eight, For you do not know what evil will be on the earth," investments are allowed, sharing gains and/or bearing losses all together.

(5) **Drug addict or Alcoholic** – Like the natural law to reap whatever we sow, the spiritual law either to reap corruption of the flesh when we sow to our flesh or to reap everlasting life of the Spirit when we sow to the Spirit (Galatians 6:8). For example, heroin or alcohol a little thing out of our interest or curiosity grows to a monster. Soon we are bound to Satan. So, the drug addict or alcoholic ("not drunk with wine…be filled with the Spirit," in Ephesians 5:18) is discouraged unless either drug or alcohol is used for a medicine purpose ("use a little wine for your stomach's sake," in 1 Timothy 5:23).

Wisdom (p 56) begins in the fear of God in Proverbs 9:10, "The fear of the LORD *is* the beginning of wisdom, And the knowledge of the Holy One *is* understanding." Here the fear of God the creator is holy fear, unlike the fear of creatures in 1 John 4:18, "There is no fear in love; but perfect love casts out fear, because fear involves torment. But he who fears has not been made perfect in love."

In **sin**, there is unpardonable sin, original sin, practical sin, or occasional sin. Unpardonable sin is unbelief as "speak against the Holy Spirit" (Matthew 12:32). Original sin is Adam's sin inherited by all people in 1 John 1:8, "If we say that we have no sin, we deceive ourselves, and the truth is not in us." Practical or habitual sin is the practice of sin, not occasional sin, in 1 John 3:9, "Whoever has been born of God does not sin, for His seed remains in him; and he cannot sin, because he has been born of God." However, we as believers can be forgiven or pardoned for all sins in 1 John 1:9, "If we confess our sins, He is faithful and just to forgive us <u>our sins</u> and to cleanse us from <u>all unrighteousness</u>."

Three (3) kinds of faith (p 59) are saving faith, growing faith, and healing faith. In healing faith, there are **passive faith** & **active faith**. Our faith is often passive rather than active, because we believe that God might do it in His time. However, in active faith when God speaks to our hearts how/where/when to do <u>now</u>, we should do accordingly, i.e. our faith is activated. For example, a woman having a flow of blood for 12 years, in Luke 8:44, "came from behind and touched <u>the border of His garment</u>. And immediately her flow of blood stopped," and then Jesus said in Luke 8:48, "And He said to her, "Daughter, be of good cheer; <u>your faith</u> had made you well. Go in peace." Here, the patient's faith was activated: when she touched (how); the border of Jesus' garment (where); when Jesus came behind (when). Then, she was completely healed like Peter's shadow (Acts 5:15) and Paul's handkerchiefs or aprons (Acts 19:12).

The gift of prophecy (p 61) means usually the gift to speak forth the word of God, i.e., forth-telling, compared with fore-telling or mutual telling (p194).

Minister never means profession but servant (p 64). Laity group and priest group are divided in the Old Testament, but we sometimes misunderstood in even the New Testament age that the priest group is ministers, pastors, or professionals and the laity group is nonprofessionals not educated in any theological seminaries. In the New Testament age, all believers have the privileges to have a close relationship with God in Christ rather than the believers in the Old Testament who could go to God once a year through a high priest in light of Hebrews 7:26-27, "^{26} For such a High Priest (Christ) was fitting for us, who is holy, harmless, undefiled, separate from sinners, and has become higher than the heavens; ^{27} who does not need daily, as those high priests (in the Old Testament), to offer up sacrifices, first for his own sins and then for the people's, for this He did once for all when He offered up Himself." So, our high priest is only our Lord Jesus Christ and all of us are priests in 1 Peter 2:9, "But you are a chosen generation, a royal priesthood, a holy nation, His own special people, that you may proclaim the praises of Him who called you out of darkness into His marvelous light." Therefore, all of us including pastors or ministers are priests and Christ is our high priest, showing the misunderstanding. Therefore, in Matthew 11:11, "Assuredly, I say to you, among those born of women there has not risen one greater than John the Baptist; but he who is least in the kingdom of heaven is greater than he," we as believers in the kingdom of heaven (royal priesthood) enjoy our privileges greater than all the believers in the Old Testament – David, Solomon, Elijah, Elisha, or even John the Baptist, because of Christ.

Rulers (p 66) stated in the Bible (e.g., Romans 12:8, "He that rules (KJV)" or "He that leads (NKJV)") mean the rulers, leaders, or masters who should have servant's heart or Christ's mind (Philippians 2:5-8), ultimately governed by God. So our ruler, leader, or master is really our Lord Jesus Christ (Matthew 23:10).

Regeneration (p 68) is synonyms of conversion, indwelling the Holy Spirit or a new believer. A man composes Spirit, Soul, and Body (1 Thessalonians 5:23) but Spirit and Soul is hard to be divided unless the discerner, the word of God, "divides asunder between soul and spirit" (Hebrews 4:12). The view after the division is called as **trichotomy** (3 parts), while before the division it is called as **dichotomy** (2 parts).

Our vital relationship (p 73) with Christ is essential because the source of all our fruit (love), spiritual nourishment, and spiritual energy are the Spirit of Christ. Our vital relationship is interchangeably used with our intimate relationship, lovely relationship, or close and beautiful fellowship with the Lord Jesus Christ (1 John 1:3).

(2) Why Grace Change Everything
(P 76-87)

Guidance

What grace is and how the grace can change our lives are guided.

Q & A

(1) How can I define "grace?"

Grace can be defined as God's freely given unmerited favor.

(2) What do I have the two aspects of the gospel of grace?

Because of our faith in Jesus Christ, all of our sins have been forgiven and God looks at us as righteous.

(3) How can I explain the Siamese twins of the New Testament?

The Siamese twins of the New Testament are "grace and peace" in that order.

(4) How can I overcome Satan's condemnation?

Satan's condemnation based upon his looking into each of us might be true. But we should respond to him, "Upon our belief in Jesus Christ God has imputed His righteousness to us."

(5) How can I strengthen the Spirit and walk in the Spirit?

We can do so by allowing the Holy Spirit to feed our Spirit into the Word of God more and more and to exercise control over our lives.

(6) What are three promises of blessings to Abraham? How can I have those promises?

They upon Abraham's belief are (1) his exceedingly great reward & God as his shield, (2) exceeding fruits, and (3) an everlasting covenant to be God between God and he and <u>his seed</u> after him, in their generations. Upon belief in Christ, his seed, all blessings are ours.

(7) Can I live a life that pleases God by own efforts? What's result?

We can't live our lives that please God by own efforts, resulting in our utterly powerless or empty lives, because we all are incapable of living righteously.

(8) Can I be justified by my good works?

No, justification by good works is impossible because it relies upon imperfect human efforts.

(9) How can I exercise my freedom of Christ?

To stand fast on the truth of God's word is the only way to maintain the glorious liberty provided to us so abundantly in Christ.

(10) What is the best safeguard against cults?

The best safeguard against cults is to (1) prove all things and (2) hold fast on which is good, <u>searching the Scriptures</u>.

Supplement

God "**accepts me as I am**" (p 78) upon my faith in Christ. God accepts what I am, not what I have done, not requiring my merits but faith alone. Because of my belief and trust in God, His grace and forgiveness are given into my life.

Satan's accusation (p 78) – One believer tempted, not possessed, by Satan might accuse another believer. Then, in the same way as Satan's accusation, only upon faith in Jesus Christ is needed because Christ's righteousness is imputed to us upon the faith, although the accusation against us is true.

Not pursuing anything (p 82) is our freedom in Christ. The term of "pursue," "try," "push," "insist," or "make an effort" is used as human efforts, without the Spirit's work -- to let the Spirit exercise control over our lives. However, for the spiritual work, the term of "lead (Romans 8:14; Matthew 4:1)," "come (Luke 1:35)," "drive (Mark 1:12)," or "descend (Matthew 3:16)" as well as in page 48 "speak (Acts 13:12)," "intercede (Romans 8:26)," "teach (John 14:26)," "commune (2 Corinthians 13:14)," "strive (Genesis 6:3)," "work miracles (Romans 15:19)," or "guide (Acts 16:6-7)" is used.

(3) The Tribulation and the Church
(P 88-94)

Guidance

Depending upon literal or non-literal interpretation of the word of God, the view of apocalypse is so different. Here, literal interpretation in the whole the Bible is guided.

Q & A

(1) Do I believe to be caught up with the Lord in heaven?

As long as we believe the Word of God is true, we should believe to be caught up with the Lord in heaven according to 1 Thessalonians 4:15-17 & 1 Corinthians 15:51-52.

(2) When is Jesus coming again? Am I ready for His coming?

Although we don't know exact time when Jesus is coming again, we should be ready for His coming because He is coming again at an hour we don't expect (Matthew 24:36, 44; 1 Thessalonians 5:7-8)

(3) Is my life changed upon faith of Jesus' 2nd coming soon in Matthew 24:44? How is it changed?

Upon the faith of Jesus' 2nd coming soon, our life is changed as (1) we can be raptured during our life; (2) we can have a constant exceeding hope to meet our Lord soon, joyfully; (3) we are constrained with AGAPE to preach to unbelievers more and more before His urgent coming; (4) The priority of our life is always the kingdom of God or eternal thing over temporary or earthly thing; (5) we are purified or sanctified to the image of Christ who is coming soon.

Supplement

Four living creatures (p 88) are stated in Revelation 4:7, "The first living creature *was* like a lion, the second living creature like a calf, the third living creature had a face like a man, and the fourth living creature *was* like a flying eagle."

April 6, 32 AD (p 89) was Christ's triumphal entry in Jerusalem (Matthew 21:1-11; Luke 19:28-40). "AD" (ANNO DOMINI The Latin)" means "after the birth of Christ" while "BC" (Before Christ)" means "before the birth of Christ," although the actual birth of Christ was earlier than "0" AD.

The church age between the 69 and 70 week of the Daniel's prophecy (p89) is the time when the Spirit of Christ has built His church with whoever believes in the Lord Jesus Christ as only savior before the Great Tribulation, the 70th week.

When the church has been removed from the earth into heaven with the Lord (rapture), **the Spirit who now restrains** (p 90) is not on the earth, also stated in Romans 11:25, "For I do not desire, brethren, that you should be ignorant of this mystery, lest you should be wise in your own opinion, that blindness in part has happened to Israel until the fullness of the Gentiles has come in." In the church age, God says in Revelation 2:7; 2:11; 2:17; 2:29; 3:6; 3:13; and 3:22, "He who has an ear, let him hear what the Spirit says to the churches." But in the Great Tribulation on the earth, God says in Revelation 13:9, "If anyone has an ear, let him hear," showing that the Spirit is not on the earth.

In **the 70th week**, 144,000 Jews (p 90) are all the twelve tribes of Israel, i.e., "12,000 per each tribe," in Revelation 7:5-8. In the Church age, when Gentiles' salvation is mainly concerned, today, if Jews accept the Lord Jesus Christ as their savior, they are saved as Gentile believers. Likewise, during the Great Tribulation period to be, when Jews' salvation is mainly concerned, if Gentile unbelievers will refuse to worship the anti-Christ and to take a mark, they will be beheaded and martyred for the witnesses to Christ, and they might be saved as 144,000 beheaded Jews do so in light of Revelation 7:14, "And I said to him, "Sir, you know." So he said to me, "These are the ones who come out of the great tribulation, and washed their robes and made them white in the blood of the Lamb," and of Revelation 20:4, "And I saw thrones, and they sat on them, and judgment was committed to them (The 1st group of raptured church, both mainly Gentile believers and Jew believers in the Church age). Then *I saw* the souls of those who had been beheaded for their witness to Jesus and for the word of God, (The 2nd group of beheaded believers, both mainly the 144,000 Jews and the Gentiles in the Great Tribulation period) who had not worshiped the beast or his image, and had not received *his* mark on their foreheads or on their hands. And they lived and reigned with Christ for a thousand years."

The Church comes back to earth riding **on white horses with Jesus Christ** (p 90) is known as Christ's coming again on the earth, stated in Revelation 19:11-16. So, the rider on the white horse in Revelation 19:11, "Now I saw heaven opened, and behold, a white horse. And He who sat on him *was* called Faithful and True, and in righteousness He judges and makes war," is Jesus Christ. However, the rider on the white horse seen during the Great Tribulation, in Revelation 6:2, "And I looked, and behold, a white horse. He who sat on it had a bow; and a crown was given to him, and he went out conquering and to conquer," is a false Messiah, a deceiver, or the anti-Christ of power.

Anti-Christ's mark or "his mark" (p 91) is stated in Revelation 13:17-18, "and that no one may buy or sell except one who has the mark or the name of the beast, or the number of his name. [18] Here is wisdom. Let him who has understanding calculate the number of the beast, for it is the number of a man: His number *is* 666."

1,290 days (p 92) are 30 days (for judgment) more than 3 ½ years while 1,335 days is 75 days (for functioning millennial kingdom) more than 3 ½ years, stated in Daniel 12:11-12, "And from the time *that* the daily *sacrifice* is taken away, and the abomination of desolation is set up, *there shall be* one thousand two hundred and ninety days. [12] Blessed *is* he who waits, and comes to the one thousand three hundred and thirty-five days."

Any exact time for rapture (p 93) - we sometimes listen to a particular date when Jesus is coming again by people who claim by themselves Christians, pastors, or prophets. Those are false teachers because they teach contrary to Jesus' teaching in Matthew 24:36 "But of that day and hour no one knows, not even the angels of heaven, but My Father only."

In Jeremiah 23, it can be exposed that there are **4 types of false teachers**. In the verses 1 through 4, God warned the pastors against destroying and scattering His sheep. Then, God continually warned false prophets against false delivering of His word, i.e. false teaching. In verse

13. ""And I have seen folly in the prophets of Samaria: They prophesied by Baal And caused My people Israel to err," the 1st type of false teacher is teaching other god's word (here Baal – knowledge idol) rather than God's word. In verse 16, "Thus says the LORD of hosts: "Do not listen to the words of the prophets who prophesy to you. They make you worthless; They speak a vision of their own heart, Not from the mouth of the LORD," the 2nd type of false teacher is teaching his own vision or imagination (KJV) rather than God's word. In verse 28,"The prophet who has a dream, let him tell a dream; And he who has My word, let him speak My word faithfully. What *is* the chaff to the wheat?" says the LORD," the 3rd type of false teacher is teaching his personal spiritual experience (here a dream like a chaff) rather than God's word (like a wheat). Refrain personal spiritual experience unless it is helpful to understand His word faithfully. Paul is good example to his spiritual experience caught up into paradise (KJV) or the third heaven (NKJV), 2 Corinthians 12:6, "For though I might desire to boast, I will not be a fool; for I will speak the truth. But I refrain, lest anyone should think of me above what he sees me *to be* or hears from me." In verse 36, "And the oracle of the LORD you shall mention no more. For every man's word will be his oracle, for you have perverted the words of the living God, the LORD of hosts, our God," the 4th type of false teacher is teaching the word of God which is perverted with human words.

Therefore, to interpret God's word faithfully we should use the Bible as the textbook (not other books with human words), our thought should be obedient to the word of God, even our spiritual experiences should be obedient to the word of God, and the entire the Bible should be observed. Here is a chart for interpretation (Hermeneutics). We adopt the literal interpretation unless a word of God as an allegoric or symbolic meaning is explained in the Bible (e.g. allegory between bond-woman and free-woman, in Galatians 4:24) because literal interpretation is firm or sound ("of a sound mind" in 2 Timothy 1:7) but non-literal interpretation is multifarious depending upon human thoughts.

Interpretation of the Bible
(Hermeneutics)

Mat 5:18; Acts 20:27; Mat 4:4; 2 Tim 3:16-17; Rev 22:18-19; Gal 4:19 ; 2 Cor 10:5

Categories		Explanation
Literal Interpretation	Historical-cultural references "God's Word & Holy Spirit" Solar Scriptura/Gratia/Fide + Solus Christus "Martin Luther" (16C)	1. Literal Interpretation : normal, plain sense including historical & grammatical references (1) figures of speech – in syntax & context (e.g. Simile, Metaphor) (2) Ordinary daily use (e.g. Webster's dictionary) 2. Historical-cultural references: root in history, cultural context of passage, & cultural relativism; Original Bible (Hebrew - OT & Greek - NT)

Non-literal Interpretation	Naturalistic "Wellhausen/Bultmann"[4] (19/20 C)	Destructive Higher Criticism	1. Naturalistic Interpretation : Anti-Supernatural 2. Destructive Higher Criticism – In no room of the Holy Spirit, criticism on the Bible in terms of history, source, form, tradition, location, or time
	Mystical or Spiritualizing, allegorizing,		e.g. evangelical mysticism (devotional meaning), e.g. psychological allegorizing (psychological principle with the Bible) *Freud*

---

[4] See http://en.wikipedia.org/wiki/Julius_Wellhausen and http://en.wikipedia.org/wiki/Rudolf_Bultmann

	Neo-Orthodoxy "experience"	1. Existentialism – existential encounter with the Word, then the Word is authoritative; the Bible contains the Word of God, not all. *Kierkegaard,[5] Barth* 2. Pragmatism – Whatever materially benefit for us, authoritative (e.g., "numbers of members vs. numbers of Saints?") 3. New Hermeneutic – seek supernatural experience through the destructive higher critical method (e.g. Salvation history) 4. Post-modernism – Postmodern Christianity, e.g. Emerging/Emergent Church (to deconstruct the meaning of the Bible and to reconstruct the meaning with postmodern thoughts "logical fallacies" *Richard Foster*

---

[5] See http://en.wikipedia.org/wiki/Kierkegaard

	Dogmatic Interpretation	Some other writings in equal authority to the Bible 1. Mormons – Book of Mormon 2. Jehovah's Witness – New World Translation of the Holy Scriptures (own translated Bible) – e.g. they are 44,000 3. Christian Science – The Key to the Scripture 4. Roman Catholicism – Church traditions + apocrypha + deviated teachings of the Bible

Interpretation theory is called as hermeneutics. In the hermeneutics of the Bible, we should adopt **literal interpretation over non-literal interpretation** because God says in Matthew 5:18, "For assuredly, I say to you, till heaven and earth pass away, one jot or one tittle will by no means pass from the law till all is fulfilled;" Acts 20:27, "For I have not shunned to declare to you the whole counsel of God;" Matthew 4:4, "But He answered and said, "It is written, 'Man shall not live by bread alone, but by every word that proceeds from the mouth of God;'"" 2 Timothy 3:16-17; "All Scripture is given by inspiration of God, and is profitable for doctrine, for reproof, for correction, for instruction in righteousness, [17] that the man of God may be complete, thoroughly equipped for every good work;" Revelation 22:18-19, "For I testify to everyone who hears the words of the prophecy of this book: If anyone adds to these things, God will add to him the plagues that are written in this book; [19] and if anyone takes away from the words of the book of this prophecy, God shall take away his part from the Book of Life, from the holy city, and *from* the things which are written in this book;" Galatians 4:19, "My little children, for whom I labor in birth again until Christ is formed in you;" 2 Corinthians 10:5, "casting down arguments and every high thing that exalts itself against the knowledge of God, bringing every thought into captivity to the obedience of Christ."

For interpretation, both literal interpretation and non-literal interpretation are existent. For **the literal interpretation**, the Bible as God's word is interpreted literally in the Holy Spirit in reference to historical-cultural consideration. It is based upon Martin Luther's allegation in 15th Century of "by scripture alone (LATIN Solar Scriputra), by grace alone (LATIN Sola Gratia), by faith alone (LATIN Solar Fide) & Christ alone (LATIN Solus Crhistus). With normal plain sense, we are using ordinary dictionaries (an English, Greek, or Hebrew dictionary) to understand the original Bible (Hebrew language in the Old Testament and Greek language in the New Testament). Figures of speech in syntax and context in the Bible itself are used with simile or metaphor, e.g., John 15:1, "I am the true vine, and My Father is the vinedresser."

For non-literal interpretation, **naturalistic interpretation** alleged by Wellhausen or Bultmann in the 19th Century is combined with destructive higher criticism. They wipe out any spiritual works in the Bible, i.e., anti-supernatural interpretation, resulting in destruction of the Word of God with critics of historical arguments or debates in an original source of books in the Bible, in dates, or in places etc.

Mystical or spiritualizing interpretation adopts a reader's own devotional meaning regardless of divine intent in the Bible itself, called as evangelical mysticism. **Allegorizing interpretation** adopts a human thought as the textbook, considering the Bible as its reference. For example, psychological allegorizing adopts the psychological principle (e.g. Freud's thoughts) as the textbook but the Bible is a mere reference book.

In **Neo-Orthodoxy interpretation**, own human experience deriving from a human thought, which they consider as a controlling factor, directs that interpretation. In **Existentialism interpretation**, when they read a word in the Bible and feel existential encounter with the word, then the word is authoritative, but words not giving any feelings to readers in the Bible are no authoritative, i.e., no God's words. In **Pragmatism interpretation**, words whichever materially benefit for me in the Bible are authoritative. The words increasing members or dollars are authoritative (i.e., result or outcome oriented interpretation), disregarding they are true believers or genuine dollars according to the Word of God.

In **New Hermeneutic interpretation**, they are seeking supernatural experience such as in their own salvation history. They interpret own salvation history as the principle to be matched with the words in the Bible – resulting in destruction of the original meaning of the Bible (destructive higher critical method) because non-matched words in the Bible are disregarded.

In **Post-modernism interpretation,** a typical one is emerging or emergent church, alleged by *Richard Foster,* seeking for their truth agreed by a participating group and so they deconstruct the meaning of the Bible and reconstruct the meaning with postmodern thoughts. Often logical fallacies come out because their meaning depends upon the participants' agreements. **Postmodernism**[6] is "a human thought after modernism." It is a skeptic thought, against modern thought called as modernism in which principles (e.g. unity, authority, certainty, objective truth, identity, etc) was previously set up, pursuing global culture narrative or association with difference or relative thoughts in most area – literary, sociology, arts, music, philosophy, politics, economics, religion and even Christianity.

In **Dogmatic interpretation,** some other writings are authoritative equal to the Bible. Mormons treats the Book of Mormon's authority equal to the Bible's, Jehovah's witnesses treat their own translated Bible as the original Bible. 44,000 in Revelation 7 stand for themselves. The key to the Scripture is controlling one to interpret the Bible in Christian Science. Roman Catholicism treats their called Pope's teaching, church tradition, and apocrypha's authority equal to the Bible's.

---

[6] See **http://en.wikipedia.org/wiki/Postmodernism**

(4) Five Points of Calvinism
(P 94-102)

Guidance

The thought of John Calvin and the thought of Jacob Hermann are compared with the Bible. And the spirit led life in all the Scripture is guided.

Q & A

(1) What does TULIP stand for?

The thought of John Calvin is described with the five (5) points – Total Depravity (T), Unconditional Election (U), Limited Atonement (L), Irresistible Grace (I), and Perseverance of the Saints (P).

(2) How can I be saved?

Since God says in Ephesians 2:8-9, "For by grace you have been saved through faith, and that not of yourselves; *it is* the gift of God, [9] not of works, lest anyone should boast," we are saved upon our faith in the Lord Jesus Christ as our savior, that is, as long as we exercise the free will given by God to accept the Lord Jesus Christ as our savior.

(3) Am I saved?

To know whether or not we are saved by God, we should examine ourselves whether or not Jesus Christ is in us <u>now</u> (2 Corinthians 13:5).

(4) Is my faith the concurrent condition for election?

Yes. Faith is the concurrent condition of conversion, regeneration, or new life because upon my faith, not after faith, regeneration starts at the same time as faith.

Supplement

In **spiritual warfare** (p 98), we should "walk not after the flesh, but after the Spirit" during our lives (Romans 8:1). That's called as "being sanctified by the Holy Spirit" (Romans 15:16). When our mind is controlled by the Spirit, we are spiritually minded. When our mind is controlled by the flesh (the body polluted with sin originated from Adam), we are fleshly/carnally minded. So, when we allow the Spirit to exercise control over our life, we can live spiritually minded life to be sanctified in the image of Christ in Romans 8:6, "For to be carnally minded is death, but to be spiritually minded is life and peace." But the terms of sanctification and salvation are used at any life time of believers on earth.

Sanctification and Salvation Terms

Life Time	General Terms	Other terms
Regeneration/ Conversion	Justification (Romans 4:25)	Positional Sanctification (Acts 20:32); Positional Salvation (Eph 2:8)
During life on earth	Sanctification (Romans 15:16)	Progressive Sanctification (Eph 5:26); Progressive Salvation (Phil 2:12)
Meeting Christ in heaven – either Rapture or Physical Death	Glorification (Romans 8:30)	Ultimate Sanctification (1 Thessalonians 5:23); Ultimate Salvation (Romans 5:10)

Salvation (p 99) requires faith alone, not work in Ephesians 2:9, "Not of works, lest any man should boast." But in James 2:3, "For as the body without the spirit is dead, so faith without works is dead also," faith naturally results in works. So, faith alone requirement for salvation suffices God's grace, which doesn't require our merit such as works. When a criminal accepted Christ just before a physical death, he was saved although he had no time to produce works naturally resulting from his faith (e.g. Luke 23:42-43 "Then he said to Jesus, "Lord, remember me when You come into Your kingdom." [43] And Jesus said to him, "Assuredly, I say to you, today you will be with Me in Paradise.").

Free will (p 99) is given to us created in His image by God in the Bible. God also states "predestination" in the Bible four (4) times – Romans 8:29, "For whom He foreknew, He also predestined to be conformed to the image of His Son, that He might be the firstborn among many brethren," Romans 8:30 "Moreover whom He predestined, these He also called; whom He called, these He also justified; and whom He justified, these He also glorified," Ephesians 1:5, "having predestined us to adoption as sons by Jesus Christ to Himself, according to the good pleasure of His will," and Ephesians 1:11, "In Him also we have obtained an inheritance, being predestined according to the purpose of Him who works all things according to the counsel of His will." But all stated predestination is only to the believers, not to the unbelievers. God chose us (believers) from beginning before we were born based upon His foreknowledge in John 15:16, "You did not choose Me, but I chose you…" God gave opportunities to be saved to all (1 John 2:2) and God knows those who will accept our Lord and be saved in advance. God chooses winners or the saved ones. So, as long as we as creatures adopt obedient thoughts to the stated predestination in the Bible, we are so thankful to the Lord to predestine us to be saved. But if we adopt framing thoughts to frame God's predestination characteristic into our human thought, e.g. God predestines some people not to be saved, we might fall into our own destruction (2 Peter 3:16) raising a lot of confusing questions – Is God good, although He predestines some people not to be saved? Do we need to preach Gospel to people, although some people are already decided not to be saved or others to be saved? Because God, creator, has foreknowledge and we, creatures, have present knowledge, we are impossible to frame or measure the uncontainable foreknowledge & predestination of God.

Dispensation (OKINOMIA the Greek) is God's special arrangement, order or plan during times, stated in Ephesians 1:10, 3:2, and Colossians 1:25. In the present time, we are in grace. We might view 2 or more up to

7 times in order to understand the Bible faithfully. But the substance is of Christ in Ephesians 1:10, "that in the <u>dispensation</u> of the <u>fullness</u> of <u>the times</u> He might gather together <u>in one all things in Christ</u>, both which are in heaven and which are on earth—in Him."

Even if we are believers, we might lose cognizable ability if we suffer **Alzheimer's disease** (p 99). Then, our capacity to exercise our free will, given by God, is taken away, like infants' capacity. We say like Job's saying in Job 1:21, "And he said: "<u>Naked</u> I came from my mother's womb, And <u>naked</u> shall I return there. <u>The LORD gave</u>, and <u>the LORD has taken away</u>; Blessed be the name of the LORD.""

Carnal Christians (p 101) will suffer a loss of rewards in the next for their works because their carnal/flesh works(not spiritual works) are burned, like wood, hay, or stubble, while Spiritual Christians will receive <u>rewards</u> for their works like gold, silver, or precious stones (1 Corinthians 3:1-15). There is the difference between spiritual works and carnal/flesh works. Carnal works are their own flesh works not controlled by the Holy Spirit.   In spiritual works, we allow the Spirit to work in us – always initiator is the Holy Spirit, who is working in us. We as respondents to the Holy Spirit do work. Those people are called as Spiritual Christians or Mature Christians. They will receive a crown, depending upon the nature of his spiritual work.

Rewards (MISTOS the Greek) as "crowns" (STEPANOS the Greek) are explained in the Bible as the following chart:

Crowns

/Five (5) Types of Crowns	The Bible
Crown of life	James 1:12 "those who love Jesus"
Incorruptible crown	1 Corinthians 9:25 "temperate in all things"
Crown of rejoicing	1 Thessalonians 2:19 (i.e. 2:9 "preaching")
Crown of righteousness	2 Timothy 4:8 "those who love His appearing"
Crown of glory	1 Peter 5:4 "shepherd" (feed His sheep)

(5) The Psychologizing of the Faith
(P 102-107)

Guidance

The difference between Psychology Counseling and Biblical Counseling is discussed. Why the Biblical Counseling is sufficient is guided.

Q & A

(1) Am I Jesus' disciple? Why?

Because Jesus says in John 8:31, "Then Jesus said to those Jews who believed Him, "If you abide in My word, you are My disciples indeed,"" we are His disciples when we abide in His word. To abide in His word, we should be taught by the Holy Spirit all things that Jesus said (John 14:26).

(2) What types of self should I deny?

We should deny self such as self-centeredness, self-righteousness, self-help, self-hope, etc.

(3) Who guides me into the truth of the Word of God?

The Holy Spirit guides us into all the truth of the Word of God.

Supplement

God's authority (p104) in the Word of God is explained as on page 169, in Matthew 28:18, "And Jesus came and spoke to them, saying, "All authority has been given to me in heaven and on earth," all authority has given to Jesus. So, the Bible which "testifies of Jesus" (John 5:39) has all authority too. The authority of Psychology is insufficient because Psychology is imperfect human thought about human mind & behaviors. But psychology might be helpful as a mere reference to understand His knowledge faithfully, like other human thoughts (e.g., psychiatrist's prescription).

(6) Calvary Chapel Distinctives
(P 108-123)

Guidance

Unique, distinct, and different Calvary Chapel from the other churches is explained, showing the balance between the teaching the Word of God and an open heart to the work of the Holy Spirit.

Q & A

(1) When I am ministering, whose is the ministry?

Because God calls us to minister to Him and His sheep, the called ministry is really His ministry, not our own ministry based upon own ambitions, own desires, and own will but upon His will, plan, aim, and purpose. We as mere instruments are used by Him for His kingdom.

(2) What are 4 basic functions of the early church? Who added the Christians to the church?

The early church had 4 basic functions – continuance of the apostles' doctrine, fellowship, breaking of bread and prayers (Acts 2:42). The Lord added the Christians to the church daily (Acts 2:47).

(3) Is the growth of a biblical church relevant to human efforts?

No. For the growth of church, the faithful ministers should get the people into the Word, in prayer, in fellowship, and in the breaking of bread. Then, God will add to the church daily such as should be saved, regardless of the human efforts to grow church.

(4) How have I experienced the Holy Spirit in three kinds?

We have experienced the Holy Spirit in 3 kinds - (1) *in*dwelling of the Holy Spirit at conversion ("en," 1 Corinthians 6:19-20), beyond the Holy Spirit dwelling **with** you ("para," John 14:16-17); (2) filled up the holy spirit or baptism with the Holy Spirit (Acts 10); (3) Overflowing with the Holy Spirit, the gift of the Spirit, or empowering of the Spirit, or the Holy Spirit **upon** you ("epi," Acts 1:8).

(5) What does "the whole counsel of God" mean to me?

"The whole counsel of God" can mean to us as "all the counsel of God" (KJV), "the whole will of God" (NIV), or "every word in the Bible."

(6) What does "the whole counsel of God" mean?

"Whole counsel of God" means that Church teaches its congregation members the whole Word of God as the priority of the Word, based upon verse by verse inductive expository sermon over deductive topical teaching; or that we do an inductive and expository study of every word in the Bible.

(7) Where is my sufficiency?

Our sufficiency is from God, not from anything else (2 Corinthians 3:5-6).

(8) Who can astound and beat the world?

Only God can astound and beat the world, by filling us with His Spirit, and doing mighty work through us, when we are to continue in the Spirit.

(9) What is God's supreme desire for me?

God's supreme desire for us is that we experience His love and then share that love with others because without love all the gifts and powers of the Holy Spirit are meaningless and worthless.

(10) How do I know God's direction?

To know His direction, we often should consider 3 factors – (1) 100 % God's glory; (2) applicable verses in the Bible; and (3) open circumstances.

(11) Who is really working in me to venture out in faith?

God. When the Holy Spirit wants to be working in us, we are not afraid to venture in faith (e.g., Acts 16:9-10).

Supplement

Calvary Chapel's model (p 109) is the early church in the Book of Acts. Therefore, Calvary Chapel doesn't belong in any denominational churches (e.g. Methodist, Pentecostal, Baptist, Presbyterian, Reformed, Lutheran, Catholic, etc.) occurred as of Roman Emperor Constantine's declaration of Christianity as the National Religion in 313 AD, in light of Christ's revelation of "...not found your works perfect before God" of the church in Sardis (Revelation 3:2, "protestant churches" in the view of church history) and "to eat things sacrificed into idols" of the church in Thyatira (Revelation 2:20, "Catholic churches" in the view of church history). But Calvary Chapel church neither opposes nor supports any denominational churches because Christ's love is supreme. But in the following time table of church history, the occurrence of Calvary Chapel in 1965 falls into the protestant time, being understood as a protestant church by the general public. But in reality Calvary Chapel belongs in neither any protestant churches nor Catholic churches (i.e., Roman and Greek[7] Catholic Churches), but to Christ Himself. Please note that the time table is a mere reference tool to understand the word of God faithfully, not the substance of Christ.

---

[7] See http://www.differencebetween.net/miscellaneous/religion-miscellaneous/differences-between-the-roman-catholic-and-greek-orthodox-churches/#ixzz1MS6c5EAv: "Greek Catholic Church" called as "Greek Orthodox Church" or "Eastern Orthodox Church"

Time Table of Church History [8]

Date	Events
2000 BC	Abraham
1446 BC	Exodus
1050 BC	Monarchy Begins (king Saul)
931 BC	Kingdom Divided Between Judah & Israel
722 BC	Assyria conquered Israel
586 BC	Babylon conquered Judah
536 BC	Persia conquered Babylon
331 BC	(1) Greece conquered Judah (2) Septuagint - a translation of the Hebrew Old Testament into the Greek in Alexandria, by 70 Jews (285-247 BC)
168 BC	(1) Abomination of Desolation (King Antiochus) – the rebel of Maccabees, Jewish army, established by the 5 sons of priest Mattathias; declaration of independence (167- 63 BC) - Feast of Dedication to purify & rededicate the Temple known as "Hanukkah" (explained below p 92). (2) Apocrypha (14 books, 3rd to 1st centuries BC) & other writings (between 2nd century BC and the 1st century AD)
27 BC	Augustus became first Roman emperor
63 BC	Rome conquered Judah

---

[8] Henry H Halley, "Halley's Bible Handbook," (Michigan; Zondervan, 1965).

4 BC	Birth of Christ
(1) Tiberius (12-37 AD) - in his reigns, Christ was crucified. (2) Nero (54-68 AD) - Executed Paul & Peter.	
14 AD	Tiberius succeeded Augustus as Roman emperor
26 AD	Pontius Pilate was appointed governor of Judea
27-28 AD	John the Baptist preached; Jesus was baptized.
29-33 AD	Jesus preached and taught. He was crucified under Pilate. The Holy Spirit came on believers on Pentecost.
35 AD	Stephen, a follower of Jesus, was stoned to death for blasphemy, becoming the 1st Christian martyr.
45 AD	Paul began to preach and teach.
49 AD	Council at Jerusalem (Acts 15), presided by James as bishop, established the precedent for addressing Church dispute of "circumcision."
60 AD	The term "Christian" was in common use. Synoptic Gospels were written.
64 AD	Roman emperor Nero blamed Christians for the Great Fire which destroyed much of Rome; and persecution ensured. Paul and Peter (perhaps) were martyred in Rome.
70 AD	Fall of Jerusalem (Titus)

(1) Domitian(81-96 AD) banished John to Patmos + 40,000 Christians martyred
(2) Trajan (98-117 AD) severely prosecuted.
(3) Diocletian (284-305 AD) the last imperial persecution
(4) The Catacombs of Rome (8 to 10 feet wide; 4 to 6 feet high ; hundreds of miles long ; about 2 million to 7 million Christians' graves

95 AD	Book of Revelation written.
313 AD	(1) Constantine (306-337 AD) [9]- on "His Edict of Toleration," declared the freedom of religion ; a general exhortation of Christianity (2) Theodosius (378-398 AD[10]) - made Christianity the State Religion of Roman Empire
395 AD	Division of Roman Empire - Eastern Empire & Western Empire
440-461 AD	(1) Leo I - 1st Pope - (some historians - "Papa" or "Father" used to all Western Bishops. Restricted to the Bishop of Rome (about 500 AD)) Developed it as Authority over Whole Church, called as "Catholic" church. (2) By the end of the 4th century - 5 large bishops (patriarchs) Rome, Constantinople, Antioch, Jerusalem, and Alexandria
476 AD	Western Roman Empire fell, empowered by

---

[9] See http://en.wikipedia.org/wiki/Constantine_the_Great

[10] See http://en.wikipedia.org/wiki/Theodosius_I - different reign time (379-395).

	Catholics in the bishop of Rome.
817 AD	Indulgence began with paganism or politics
1453 AD	Eastern Roman Empire fallen by Turks (Moslem country) that ruled Constantinople. All Catholics in the other 4 bishops rather than Rome bishop were empowered by Moslem (the 2nd threat of Moslem controlling against Europe, which, later was stopped by John Sobieski in the battle of Vienna (1683 AD), leaving the Greek Catholics today.)
1517 AD	Protestants (Martin Luther, John Calvin, John Knox, Roger Williams, John Wesley, etc)
1965 AD	Calvary Chapel (Chuck Smith[11])

The Lord added to the church daily those whoever being saved (p109) shows **success**. Success means "to gain an aim." The issue is whose aim: God's aim or our earthly aim? To have done what God wants or to have done what we want? We think often that success is to gain "wealth," "long life or longevity," and "fame" on the earth. In Hebrews 11, it is discovered that very few of them got them (e.g. Abraham or Noah) but most of them did not get them. How about Jesus' disciples? Most of them were killed for their faith except John (but banished to Patmos, Revelation 1:9). Paul was also killed for his faith. Jesus Himself was killed on the cross for us. John, Peter, or Paul might have gotten fame but all the other people were far from such earthly success. Further, the seven churches in Revelation 2 and 3 do not exist today at all in Turkey, i.e., no longevity. In view of church history, the church of the Laodiceans was earthly

---

[11] See http://calvarychapelcostamesa.com/about/history

successful, but was scold, by Christ, of "Because you say, '<u>I am rich</u>, have <u>become wealthy</u>, and <u>have need of nothing</u>'—and do not know that you are <u>wretched, miserable, poor, blind, and naked</u>—(Revelation 3:17)." However, the church in Philadelphia, which had a little strength, "…you have <u>a little strength</u>, have kept My word, and have not denied My name (Revelation 3:8b)," was commended for "Behold, I am coming quickly! Hold fast what you have, that no one may take <u>your crown</u> (Revelation 3:11)." Therefore the success in the point of God is to gain a divine aim or to have done what God wants, regardless of gaining our earthly aim. Such prosperity as "wealth," "long life or longevity," and "fame" as the result, not gaining or pursuing our earthly aim, may be given alone by God, like Abraham; Solomon who asked only wisdom to discern justice but was given "not-asked riches and honor" by God in 1 Kings 3:4-14.

Therefore, here the added saints to the church was just the result from the early church believers who had done what the Spirit of God wanted the 4 basic functions (continuance of the apostles' doctrine, fellowship, breaking of bread, and prayers), not pursuing the increase of members as their earthly aim with the flesh efforts of fund raising, marketing, star shows, coercive sermons, or competition. Here are successful stories in the point of God such as Jeremiah's ministry (Jeremiah 7:27, "Therefore <u>you shall speak all these words to them</u>, but they will not obey you. You shall also call to them, but <u>they will not answer you</u>" (Jeremiah had done what God wanted although nobody answered him)) or Peter's sermon (Acts 2:41, "Then <u>those who gladly received his word were baptized</u> (Peter had done what the Spirit of God wanted to teach and baptize); and that day <u>about three thousand souls</u> were added *to them*"(the increase given solely by God)) or <u>growing word</u> (Acts 12:24, "But the word of God grew and multiplied" (the

Spirit of God fed their spirit into the Word of God)) or <u>AGAPE fruit</u> (John 15:5 "I am the vine, you are the branches. He who abides in Me, and I in him, <u>bears much fruit</u>; for <u>without Me you can do nothing</u>" (the fruit without Christ can't be produced) regardless of the "increase" but up to God (1 Corinthians 3:7, "So then neither he who plants is anything, nor he who waters, but <u>God who gives the increase</u>)." Here, the increase with our flesh efforts are not accounted at all for **the success of believers** in light of 1 Timothy 1:1, "…the Lord Jesus Christ, our hope." Therefore, our success is to gain God's aim or to have done what God wants.

In **the priority of the word** (p112), the word of God is prior to even His name in Psalm 138:2, "I will worship toward Your holy temple, And praise Your name For Your lovingkindness and Your truth; For You have <u>magnified Your word above all Your name</u>." **The "inductive and expository study"** means that, without human pre-conceived thoughts, let every word in the Bible lead us to understand, i.e., let the Holy Spirit teach us every word in the Bible.

In **the supremacy of love** (p 114), is the **capital punishment** or death penalty prohibited to any homicide cases in the point of God?   No.   God's love "does not rejoice in iniquity" (1 Corinthians 13:6a). So, God "hates all workers of iniquity" (Psalm 5:5b). God hates all sinners unless they repent their sin. God says in Genesis 9:6, "Whoever sheds man's blood, By man his blood shall be shed; For in the image of God He made man." Therefore, the slayer of an innocent man is subject to capital punishment or death penalty because the victim was made in the image of God.

The **100% God's glory** (p 121) is the first element to discern God's direction with the other 2 elements -- applicable verses in the Bible and open Circumstances. The first element is often tainted with not only self glories but also with the love of money in light of 2 Timothy 3:2, "For men will be <u>lovers of themselves</u>, <u>lovers of money</u>, boasters, proud, blasphemers, disobedient to parents, unthankful, unholy" in the last days. The love of money is a root of all kinds of evil in 1 Timothy 6:10, "For <u>the love of money</u> is <u>a root of all *kinds of* evil</u>, for which some have strayed from the faith in their <u>greediness</u>, and pierced themselves through with many sorrows." We saw Judas Iscariot's allegation to sell the very costly ointment of spikenard and to care for the poor (rather than to anoint upon the feet of Jesus) appeared for God's glory through the charity. But Jesus said in John 12:6, "This he said, <u>not that he cared for the poor</u>, but because <u>he was a thief</u>, and had the money box; and he used to take what was put in it." We should pray to the Lord to reveal our hearts, anything else other than 100% God's glory, the love of God, or the Kingdom of God. Otherwise, we might be devoured by the devil in 1 Peter 5:8, "Be sober, be vigilant; because your adversary the devil walks about like <u>a roaring lion</u>, seeking whom he may <u>devour</u>." Please note that money per se is nothing evil but the love of money is evil. Further Jesus asks us to manage money itself well for God's glory in light of Luke 14:28," For which of you, intending to build a tower, does not sit down first and <u>count the cost</u>, whether he has *enough* to finish *it*," and Luke 16:11, "Therefore if you have not been <u>faithful in the unrighteous mammon</u> [money], who will commit to your trust the true *riches?*' So, **tithes, offerings, revenues, expenses** (see page 137: feeding sheep, mission, charity, and ministers), or **taxes** should be wisely managed according to the State and Federal law within the scope of the word of God ("Render therefore to all their due: taxes to whom taxes *are due*," in Romans 13:1-7; "Render therefore to Caesar the things that are Caesar's, and to God the things that are God's" in Matthew 22:20-21).

(7) Second
(P 124-131)

Guidance

The second's role is explained to serve his master whose ultimate master is our Lord Jesus Christ in the Scriptural view.

Q & A

(1) What do "the second" and "the mentor" mean? What is the difference between a hireling and the second?

The "second" and "mentee" terms are synonyms, while the "mentor" and "master" terms are synonyms.   The second or mentee is humbly assisting his master or mentor while his master or mentor is influencing, affecting, and impacting on him to multiply ministries in light of the characteristics described in the Bible.

When anyone is hired to do it by the board or somebody, he is called to be a hireling. But a believer to be delegated to serve Him and His sheep (the congregation members) by God is called to be the second.

(2) Who sandpapers my ego?

God sandpapers our ego.

Supplement

"**A master**" (p 127) and "purchased with His own blood" (p129) are used. We are purchased by our Lord Jesus Christ with His blood shed (1 Corinthians 6: 19-20). We are not ours but Christ's. So, our ultimate master is really Christ as stated in Matthew 23:10(KJV), "Neither be ye called masters: for one is your Master, even Christ." Here our master is Christ, although we often call our direct ruler or leader as a master, within the scope of God's Word and limited to his physical life. So, he also as a mere instrument of Christ is ruling or leading us for His kingdom as we as the instruments are assisting him for His kingdom.

<u>Videos</u>:

(1) *A Venture in Faith*
(P 131-140)

Guidance

What is "a venture in faith" is defined. Whenever God begins to work, how we should respond to Him is guided. Chuck gave examples out of his life experiences to make us understand and to apply the venture in faith to our lives for His glory and kingdom.

Q & A

(1) How much should I depend upon God during my life?

We should depend totally upon God during our lives as much as we can.

(2) Why can I frustrate a ministry?

Because the ministry comes from a man's leading rather than God's leading.

(3) What is difference between Charismatic movement and Charismatic church?

In charismatic movement, our heart is open to the flexible work of the gifts of the Holy Spirit upon our belief in the validity of gifts of the Holy Spirit, verified by the Word of God. But in charismatic church the apparent works of the Holy Spirit are not often verified by the Word of God but controlled capriciously by human emotions.

(4) Who is my initiator to live?

An initiator should be God in Romans 8:14.

(5) Do I apply faith wherever I go?

We should apply faith wherever we go, reflecting our full trust in the Lord to be conformed into His image.

(6) Am I given freedom by whom? To whom am I responsible?

We are given freedom by God who guides us. Also we are responsible to God.

(7) What destroy my ministry to the Lord?

An ivy tower, institutionalization, and 3 G (abbreviated girl, gold, and girl terms) destroy the ministry to the Lord, not out of the work of the Spirit.

Supplement

A big **Ivy tower, institutionalization, and the love of girl, gold, and glory** (p139) simply come from our flesh, so that they would destroy the ministry ordained and controlled by the Holy Spirit.

(2) How and Why Series
(P 140-148)

Guidance

Church Dedication, Communion Service, Baptism, Marriage, and Baby Dedication are discussed and guided.

Q & A

(1) Did I participate in Church dedication, communion service, water baptism, wedding service, and/or baby dedication?

We probably participated in Church dedication, which means "a facility where we serve dedicated to God." Communion service is a memorial service to remind us the past event of Jesus Christ in light of suffering, love, and sin. Water baptism is publicly acknowledged that old life is dead and new life in the unity of Jesus Christ is born again. In wedding service, both groom and bride come side by side before God to join Husband and Wife who have the most intimate relationship. In baby dedication, parents make a decision or vow to dedicate the baby's life to the Lord, based upon their faith.

(2) Does God see my whole picture for eternal plan?

Of course, yes. But our whole pictures for eternal plans are in diversity to each of us for divine Kingdom & His glory. Looking back each own biography, through prayer each of us could see a unique & distinctive whole picture for eternal plan.

(3) What does communion service mean to me?

For each of us, Jesus Christ was dead with His broken body in the unity of us to His Body & with His blood shed to cleanse away our sins.

(4) What does Christ's saying to "Take My yoke upon you" mean to me?

It means "let Christ direct our life."

(5) In the wedding what does "the exchange of rings" mean to the couples?

Each exchanges rings symbolizing "eternity, love, and pledge."

(6) What are two aspects that the memorial service has?

The memorial service has two aspects – one is memorial and the other is eternity.

(7) What are two types of death?

One is the physical death - the separation of the consciousness from the body or the separation of spirit from your body, while the other one is the spiritual death, the separation of man's consciousness from God, e.g., physical life only for his pleasure but his spiritual death.

(8) When can I have a water baptism ceremony before the public?

When we believe in our Lord Jesus Christ as our savior, we can have a water baptism anytime before the public.

Supplement

Communion service (p 142) is originated from the Lord's Supper or the Last Supper (Luke 22:15-20, see above). Breaking bread is a symbol of Christ's broken body on the cross for us (1 Corinthians 11:24). So when we take a piece of the bread and eat it, each of us is a part of His body, i.e., the unity of the Body of Christ. Taking the cup is a symbol of Christ's blood shed on the cross for us (1 Corinthians 11:25). So when we take the cup, our sins are cleansed away with His blood shed. To remind us the past event of death of Jesus Christ, we often participate in the Communion Service.

Marriage (p 144) is ordained by God as long as husband and wife are believers. So, **sexual relationship** as of marriage between one husband and one wife is ordained by God in light of Genesis 2:24, "Therefore a man shall leave his father and mother and be joined to his wife, and they shall become one flesh." Since Jesus' love is a key element between husband and wife like the Lord Jesus Christ and His church (Ephesians 5:22, 25), sexual relationship ought to be based upon mutual consent, being kept secret in light of Ephesians 5:32, "This is a great mystery, but I speak concerning Christ and the church." We as husband and wife should handle together each natural sexual desire given by God not tempted to sexual immorality by Satan, in 1 Corinthians 7:5, "Do not deprive one another except with consent for a time, that you may give yourselves to fasting and prayer; and come together again so that Satan does not tempt you because of your lack of self-control." **Procreation** also is blessed in Genesis 1:28, "Then God blessed them, and God said to them, "Be fruitful and multiply; fill the earth and subdue it; have dominion over the fish of the sea, over the birds of the air, and over every living thing that moves on the earth." However, **cohabitation without marriage** ("sexual immorality," in Matthew 5:32), **same gender marriage** ("gave them up unto vile affections," in Romans 1:26-27), and **adultery**

which is defined as sexual relationship with another rather than his or her own spouse, ("shall not commit adultery" in Exodus 20:14) are prohibited. Abortion as discussed above is discouraged with rare exceptions. **Contraception** among married couple is okay because a fetus or person is not formed yet (Jeremiah 1:5).

In the New Testament, **polygamy** is discouraged in Matthew 19:4-5, "And He answered and said to them, "Have you not read that He who made *them* at the beginning *'made them male and female,'* [5] and said, *'For this reason a man shall leave his father and mother and be joined to his wife, and the two shall become one flesh'*?" and is considered as adultery "to have sexual relationship with other(s) than another spouse." **Pornography** are considered as "adultery" in light of Matthew 5:27-28, "You have heard that it was said to those of old, *'You shall not commit adultery.'* [28] But I say to you that whoever looks at a woman to lust for her has already committed adultery with her in his heart," and so are prohibited. Also **divorce** of believers is discouraged (see above, page 36) in light of Matthew 19:6, "So then, they are no longer two but one flesh. Therefore what God has joined together, let not man separate." Anger or wrath arising from any reasons often causes divorce. The meditation of James 1:19-20, "So then, my beloved brethren, let every man be swift to hear, slow to speak, slow to wrath; [20] for the wrath of man does not produce the righteousness of God," might help us to get along. But divorce with unbeliever is allowed only if an unbeliever spouse wants to do so in 1 Corinthians 7:15, "…if the unbeliever departs, let him depart…" but if an unbeliever spouse doesn't want to divorce, divorce is discouraged because the unbeliever might be saved in light of 1 Corinthians 7:13-14.

Cast Down Thoughts?

(P 148-163)

Guidance

The human thoughts of which we have often heard are discussed and guided according to the Word of God for preaching.

Q & A

(1) Can I put God in a man made frame?

God's knowledge should not be put in a man's frame because a finite man has a limited understanding to infinite God's knowledge, even if we don't understand (2 Peter 3:16).

(2) What is "Christian's devil possession?"

It is that a Christian may be possessed by a devil or Satan.

(3) What is difference between "the Word of Faith" and "the Venture in Faith"?

The difference is who is a master. The master of "the Word of Faith" is a believer because he thinks that whatever he wants and prays constantly, God will provide it. Here God is a mere assistant. The master of "the Venture in Faith" is God because he takes a step in faith when God wants to be working with us through His word under open circumstances.

(4) What is Prosperity Gospel?

It is the gospel that God provides His children material prosperity, wealth and physical health.

(5) What is Positive Thought doctrine?

It is a human doctrine to think of no matter what in a positive way.

(6) What is Feeling Good doctrine?

It dominates teaching and preaching to make hearers feel good such as "love," "joy," "peace," "comfort," "hope," "blessing," "mercy," "grace," "prosperity," "eternal life," "victory," and so on, while it negates "cross," "blood shed," "patience," "long suffering," "persecution," "judgment," "righteousness," "faithfulness," "humility," "many tears," and so on.

(7) What is Signs and Wonders Movement?

It is based on tongues, extreme feeling, healing, meeting a dead person, holy laughing, roaring in the spirit, extraordinary feelings, Yoga power, and peace coming from such experiences as allegedly "grace gifts," given by the Holy Spirit. Those are not verified by the Word of God but some of them are contrary to the Word of God.

(8) What is Emerging Church?

Emerging or Emergent Church appears a church who seeks to deconstruct the meaning of the Bible and to reconstruct the meaning combined with thoughts of people who live in a postmodern culture or postmodernism.

(9) What is Evolutional Creation?

God uses evolution process as a tool of God's creation.

(10) What is New Age?

It is the movement to seek for "Universal Truth" by rejecting any religious doctrine but to draw allegedly inspiration from Christianity, Buddhism, Hinduism, Islam, Judaism, Chinese folk religion with other philosophies.

(11) What is Witness Lee?

Witness Lee established Living Stream Ministry (LSM), promoting Watchman Nee - imprisoned in 1952 for his faith and dead in 1972 - who wrote "The Normal Christian Life," with the strong opposition of denominational churches.

(12) What is Messianic Jews?

They are not necessarily Jews, but they are different from both Christianity and Judaism, deriving from the both into their own faith in favor of Hebrew culture rather than western Greek culture, emphasizing the old covenantal duty of Jewish life from Torah which is the 5 books of Moses or Pentateuch.

(13) What's Seventh-day Adventists?

They believe in Trinity and infallible Bible and Jesus' 2nd coming as other biblical churches, distinctive with only Saturday service and food strictly literal application by the Old Testament, unconscious state of the dead, and the doctrine of an investigative judgment, etc.

(14) What do Catholics believe?

Catholics believe not only the Bible, not whole, but also the Roman Catholic traditions, Purgatory, Virgin Mary God the mother, apocrypha, bowed image, salvation with faith plus work, geographical culture, and so on.

(15) What is an atheist?

He is a person who thinks of the absence of god, by either rejection of god or god no existence, originated from skepticism or criticism of god.

(16) Can I see my neighbor who doesn't believe in Christ? What is his thought? Can I get a parable or an opening statement to deliver Gospel from these thoughts?

When we listen to an unbeliever neighbor humbly, we could see his thought related to the cast down thoughts. Through our silent prayers, we might be led by the Spirit to develop his interesting parable or open statement to deliver Gospel without offense in Agape love.

Supplement

Amish[12] group, called as either Amish church or Amish Mennonites church, began in 1963 by Alsatian Anabaptists in Switzerland and established in the 18th century into America. They are isolated from the world and live in their own community for a simple humble plain rural life with manual labor distinct from our modern technological life. Thus, they discontinue our formal education system at grade eight and have their own school system. The group districts are about 30 families, ruled by a bishop, ministers, and deacons. Marriage is required only among the member of the Amish group. Every other Sunday hold they worship service.

Their simple life is accepted consistent with the Bible in Romans 16:19, "For your obedience has become known to all. Therefore I am glad on your behalf; but I want you to be wise in what is good, and simple concerning evil," but is cast down within the meaning of the Bible in Proverbs 22:3 "A prudent man foresees evil and hides himself, But the simple pass on and are punished." The humble or plain life is accepted consistent with the Bible in many verses such as in James 4:1, "But He

---

[12] See http://en.wikipedia.org/wiki/Amish

gives more grace. Therefore He says: "God resists the proud, But gives grace to the humble." But their only rural life isolated from the world should be cast down, contrary to Jesus' teachings. Jesus teaches in John 17:14-17, "I have given them Your word; and the world has hated them because they are not of the world, just as I am not of the world. [15] I do not pray that You should take them out of the world, but that You should keep them from the evil one. [16] They are not of the world, just as I am not of the world. [17] Sanctify them by Your truth. Your word is truth" and in Matthew 5:13-14, "You are the salt of the earth; but if the salt loses its flavor, how shall it be seasoned? It is then good for nothing but to be thrown out and trampled underfoot by men. [14] You are the light of the world. A city that is set on a hill cannot be hidden." So, we are not of the world but live in the world to be sanctified by His word and to be the salt and light of the earth. Therefore, we may choose either rural or urban life, but not isolated from the world, although we are of heaven.

Marriage requirement only among the member of the Amish group should be cast down, inconsistent with Jesus teaching in Matthew 19:10-12 "His disciples said to Him, "If such is the case of the man with *his* wife, it is better not to marry." [11] But He said to them, "All cannot accept this saying, but only *those* to whom it has been given: [12] For there are eunuchs who were born thus from *their* mother's womb, and there are eunuchs who were made eunuchs by men, and there are eunuchs who have made themselves eunuchs for the kingdom of heaven's sake. He who is able to accept *it,* let him accept *it."* So, for the kingdom of heaven's sake, we as believers can marry among believers, not just the Amish group, or we can live as singles.

B. Why Only The Bible?

(P 164-170)

1. The Bible can be proved to be true with following four (4) human reasons.

Guidance

God is absolutely true. So His word is absolutely true. If the Bible is His word, the Bible is also absolutely true. We as finite people can't prove the absolute truth of the Bible but with finite reasons (here 4 reasons) can prove some truth of the Bible.

Q & A

(1) Is God's truth dependent upon my wisdom or defense?

No, because God's truth is perfect, infallible, inerrant, authoritative or absolute, being independent upon our wisdom or defense. But our wisdom merely might be helpful for us to understand His truth.

(2) What do "revelation" and "inspiration" mean?

Revelation is to make us to know or disclose an unknown thing (e.g. God allows us to know His reason), while inspiration is to receive a power from God (e.g. a special meaning "God-breathed," in 2 Timothy

3:16).

(3) Which ways can I prove the Bible is true?

We can prove the Bible is true with four (4) ways – (1) a reason from science; (2) a reason from archeology; (3) a reason from fulfilled the Bible prophecy; and (4) a reason to change lives from the Bible.

(4) Are human proofs sufficient to prove "Absolute truth" of the Bible? How can I understand the Absolute Truth?

No, any human proofs are not sufficient to prove "Absolute truth" of the Bible because we can't understand the absolute truth of the Bible unless the Holy Spirit given by infinite God reveals His wisdom to us.

Supplement

Revelation (p 164) may be classified with 3 types – General Revelation, Special Revelation, and Personal or Specific Revelation. (1) **General Revelation** is shown to everybody in Romans 1:20," For since the creation of the world His invisible *attributes* are clearly seen, being understood by the things that are made, *even* His eternal power and Godhead, so that they are without excuse," the creation of the world makes everybody to know or disclose Godhead and His eternal power. (2) **Special Revelation** is shown only to believers in 1 Corinthians 2:10, "But God has revealed *them* to us through His Spirit. For the Spirit searches all things, yes, the deep things of God," and in 1 Corinthians

2:14, "But <u>the natural man does not receive</u> the things of the Spirit of God, for they are foolishness to him; nor can he know *them,* because they are spiritually discerned." And (3) **Personal or Specific Revelation** is shown to an individual or personal believer in 2 Corinthians 12:1-6 (KJV), "It is not expedient for me doubtless to glory. I will come to visions and <u>revelations of the Lord</u>. ²I knew a man in Christ above fourteen years ago, (whether in the body, I cannot tell; or whether out of the body, I cannot tell: God knoweth;) such an one <u>caught up to the third heaven</u>. ³And I knew such a man, (whether in the body, or out of the body, I cannot tell: God knoweth;) ⁴How that he was caught up into paradise, and heard unspeakable words, which it is not lawful for a man to utter. ⁵Of such an one will I glory: yet of myself I will not glory, but in mine infirmities. ⁶For though I would desire to glory, I shall not be a fool; for <u>I will say the truth</u>: but <u>now I forbear</u>, lest any man should think of me <u>above that</u> which he seeth me to be, or that he heareth of me." Here, Paul recommended that we better keep silent because any men might think more than what we saw and said, i.e., to avoid their misunderstanding.

2. Why not others than the Bible?
(P 170-182)

Guidance

To deliver Gospel to unbelievers, we can develop parables or open statements close to their thoughts from the introduced books other than the Bible.

Q & A

(1) What is Dharma? Is a Buddhist around me? Can I deliver Gospel through prayer?

Dharma is teachings of Buddha, the founder of Buddhism, about eliminating self desire, merciful charity practice, rebirth to an animal or man, etc. While we listen to our neighbor and discover that he is a Buddhist, through our silent prayers, we might be led by the Spirit to develop his interesting parable or open statement to deliver Gospel without offense in Agape love.

(2) What is Smrti? What is Vedas? Is a Hindu around me? Can I deliver Gospel through prayer?

Smrti (Remembers) is one part of Hindu's writing with Sruti (Revealed), regarding ritual/social duty, mystical contemplation, and ascetic practices. Vedas is the book of wisdom for Hindus, containing hymns, rituals, theology, and philosophy. While we listen to our neighbor and discover that he is a Hindu, through our silent prayers, we might be led by the Spirit to develop his interesting parable or open statement to deliver Gospel without offense in Agape love.

(3) What is Koran? Is a Muslim around me? Can I deliver Gospel through prayer?

Koran is the book as Allah revealed to Muhammad through the angel

Gabriel, accepted by Muslims, who must obey Allah – not trinity God but only one god. While we listen to our neighbor and discover that he is a Muslim, through our silent prayers, we might be led by the Spirit to develop his interesting parable or open statement to deliver Gospel without offense in Agape love.

(4) What is Talmud? Is a Jew around me? Can I deliver Gospel through prayer?

The book written about Jewish tradition by ancient Rabbis contains two sections of the Mishnah and the Gemara for Judaism. Majority of Jews are Judaists who are orthodox, conservative, or liberal Judaists, but Jews for Christ are Christians as we are.

While we listen to him and discover that he is a Judaist, through our silent prayers, we might be led by the Spirit to develop his interesting parable or open statement to deliver Gospel without offense in Agape love.

(5) What is Apocrypha?

Apocrypha is often the 14 books written by uncertain authors during 1st through 3rd Centuries BC, included between the Old Testament and the New Testament in Septuagint and Vulgate Bibles but excluded from the cannons of the Bible.

(6) What is "Science and Health with Key to the Scripture"? Can I deliver Gospel to the Church of Christ Scientist through prayer?

"Science and Health with Key to the Scripture" is the book written by Mary Baker Eddy founding "the Church of Christ, Scientist," often called as Christian Science, in 1879 derived from the Bible but emphasized healing through prayers in the Bible over modern medical treatment and added cause and effect science theory in the book and rejected the reality of sin, sickness, death, and the material world in the Bible. While we listen to him and discover that he is a Scientist in the Church of Christ, through our silent prayers, we might be led by the Spirit to develop his interesting parable or open statement to deliver Gospel without offense in Agape love.

(7) What is the Book of Mormon? Can I deliver Gospel to a Mormon through prayer?

The Book of Mormon was published with the use of Mormon the prophet not in the Bible in 1830 by Joseph Smith, Jr. Mormons practice the book of Mormon in the name of (1) the Church of Jesus Christ of Latter-day Saints (LDS church), (2) Mormon fundamentalists who are still practicing polygamy, or (3) Community of Christ (e.g. Adam-God doctrine; Jesus born of a virgin, not conceived by the Holy Spirit; Polygamy; Marriage life resurrected after physical death; Salvation comes by faith with human efforts), with the Bible in part. While we listen to him and discover that he is a Mormon, through our silent prayers, we might be led by the Spirit to develop his interesting parable or open statement to deliver Gospel without offense in Agape love.

(8) What is New World Translation of the Holy Scriptures? Can I deliver Gospel to a Jehovah's Witness through prayer?

New World Translation of the Holy Scriptures were translated by the Watch Tower Society of Jehovah's Witnesses, founded by Charles Russell and Judge Rutherford, is different from the Bible (e.g. denying the divinity of Christ and alleging that Jesus Christ is a spirit and archangel Michael before being born; eternal life on earth; when Jesus came to earth from heaven, He laid aside angelic (or spiritual) nature and lived as a man and when He left earth, He laid aside his human nature; 144,000 are Jehovah's Witnesses in the Book of Revelation; Refusal of blood transfusions, etc.) While we listen to him and discover that he is a Jehovah's Witness, through our silent prayers, we might be led by the Spirit to develop his interesting parable or open statement to deliver Gospel without offense in pure Agape lovely broken heart.

Supplement

The **Apocrypha**[13] usually known as the 14 books (I Esdras; II Esdras; Tobit; Judith; Rest of Esther; Wisdom of Solomon; Ecclesiasticus; Baruch; Song of the Three Holy Children; History of Susanna; Bell and the Dragon; Prayer of Manasses; I Maccabees; and II Maccabees) in the 1st to the 3rd centuries BC, between the Old and New Testaments, added to the Septuagint, the Roman Catholic Bible (Vulgate the Bible), but not added to the Bible because they were never quoted by Jesus nor

---

[13] Henry H. Halley, (Ibid.).

found in the Hebrew Old Testament, i.e., lack of Divine Authority of God's Word. But the books of I Maccabees and II Maccabees as references are helpful to understand Jewish history as in the 2nd century BC, Mattathias (See above, page 65), a Jewish priest, and his five sons gathered a Jewish army, called as Maccabees. The army rebelled and battled against King Antiochus who prohibited their worship in the temple of Jerusalem rather than put the pagan god, Zeus, and used pigs as sacrifice in the temple (called as "abomination of desolation"), winning the battle. And the army purified and rededicated the temple to our Lord. Today, Jewish people celebrated this event for 8 days in the name of HANUKKAH (meaning "feast of dedication").

Other apocryphal books began in the 2nd Century are Gospel of Nicodemus, Protevangelium of James, Passing of Marry, Gospel according to the Hebrews, Gospel of the Ebionites, Gospel of the Egyptians, Gospel of Peter, Gospel of Pseudo-Matthew, Gospel of Thomas, Gospel of Judas, Nativity of Mary, Arabic Gospel of the Childhood, Gospel of Joseph the Carpenter, Anpocalypse of Peter, Acts of Paul, Acts of Peter, Acts of John, Acts of Andrew, Acts of Thomas, Letter of Peter to James, The Epistle from Laodicea, Letters of Paul to Seneca, or The Abgarus Letters.

All are cast down in light of "...shall not add to the word..." in Deuteronomy 4:2 and "...if any man shall add unto these things, God shall add unto him the plagues..." in Revelation 22:18.

1. Faith Statement

(P 183-192)

Guidance

What we believe is stated, called as "Faith Statement," "the Statement of Faith," or "Doctrinal Belief," falling into evangelical, conservative, or biblical churches.

Q & A

(1) What does Trinity mean?

Trinity means three ones in one. Trinity God is one God in three persons – the Father, Son, and Holy Spirit who are coeternal, coequal, and coexistent (Matthew 3:16-17; Genesis 1:26).

(2) What does Deity mean?

Deity means God. Jesus Christ is the Son of God (John 1:34; John 1:49).

(3) Did Jesus resurrect?

Yes (1 Corinthians 15:4).

(4) How can I be saved?

Upon our faith alone in the Lord Jesus Christ as our savior (Ephesians 2:8-9), we can be saved from eternal death.

(5) What's the present ministry of the Spirit?

Our present ministries are in diversity and in a unique way, being called by God (e.g. teaching ministry, pastoral ministry, charity ministry, preaching ministry, etc.)

(6) What's difference between the gifts and the fruit of the Spirit?

The gifts of the Spirit are given by the Spirit in 1 Corinthians 12:8-10 & Romans 12:5-8 (e.g. wisdom, knowledge, discerning of spirits, faith, healings, miracles, prophecy, tongues, interpretation of tongues, ministry, teaching, exhortation, giving with liberality, leading with diligence, and mercy with cheerfulness), while the fruit of the Spirit is Agape love described as several attributes in Galatians 5:22-23 (8 terms – joy, peace, long suffering, kindness, goodness, faithfulness, gentleness, and self-control) and 1 Corinthians 13:4-8 (e.g. suffers long, kind, etc.).

(7) Is my life fruitful for Jesus Christ? Am I fruitful for the Kingdom of God? Is the fruit of the Spirit coming forth from my life?

The fruit of our life is Agape love. When we examine ourselves whether or not Agape love is existent in our ministries during our lives, we can see the fruit of the Sprit coming forth from our lives.

(8) Am I in the spiritual unity of believers?

We should be in the spiritual unity of believers not only of a local church but also of all the world (Ephesians 1:22-23).

(9) What do "pre-tribulation" and "pre-millennium" mean?

Pre-tribulation means "before tribulation," i.e., the rapture of the Church (all believers) will occur before Great Tribulation. Pre-millennium means "before millennium," i.e., the rapture of Church will occur before the Millennium Kingdom established by Christ who will return on earth.

Supplement

In the Apostles' Creed (p 185), **He descended into hell** (in 1 Peter 3:19 "by whom also He went and preached to the spirits in prison").

In Matthew 12:40, when Jesus died on the cross, Jesus was "three days and three nights in the heart of the earth (Matthew 12:40)." The heart of the earth is hell or grave. It in the Old Testament is translated as "Sheol," and it in the New Testament is translated as Hades.

Jesus said in Luke 16:19-31, "There was a certain rich man who was clothed in purple and fine linen and fared sumptuously every day. [20] But there was a certain beggar named Lazarus, full of sores, who was laid at his gate, [21] desiring to be fed with the crumbs which fell from the rich man's table. Moreover the dogs came and licked his sores. ²² So it was that the beggar died, and was carried by the angels to Abraham's bosom. The rich man also died and was buried. ²³ And being in <u>torments in Hades</u>, he lifted up his eyes and saw Abraham afar off, and Lazarus <u>in his bosom</u>. ²⁴ "Then he cried and said, 'Father Abraham, have mercy on me, and send Lazarus that he may dip the tip of his finger in water and cool my tongue; for I am tormented in this flame.' ²⁵ But Abraham said, 'Son, remember that in your lifetime you received your good things, and likewise Lazarus evil things; but now he is <u>comforted</u> and you are tormented. ²⁶ And besides all this, between us and you there is a great gulf fixed, so that those who want to <u>pass from here to you cannot</u>, nor can those from there pass to us.' ²⁷ "Then he said, 'I beg you therefore, father, that you would send him to my father's house, ²⁸ for I have five brothers, that he may testify to them, lest they also come to this place of torment.' ²⁹ Abraham said to him, 'They have Moses and the prophets; let them hear them.' ³⁰ And he said, 'No, father Abraham; but if one goes to them from the dead, they will repent.' ³¹ But he said to him, '<u>If they do not hear Moses and the prophets</u>, <u>neither will they be persuaded</u> though one rise from the dead.'"

Here Jesus told <u>the story</u> between the rich man and Lazarus, not a parable. Hades was divided into two compartments in which one was <u>torments compartment</u> and the other was <u>comfort compartment</u> in Abraham's bosom. The believers in the Old Testament as Lazarus were in the comfort compartment, while unbelievers in the Old Testament as the rich man were in the torments compartment.

In Peter 3:19, "by whom also He went and preached (KERUGMA the Greek to proclaim or announce to the believers, not EUANGELIZOU the

Greek to preach to the unbelievers) to the spirits in prison," Jesus' spirit and soul descended into Hades and announced His resurrection to the believers in the Old Testament, in the comfort compartment of the Hades, who were "all these, having obtained a good testimony through faith, did not receive the promise" (Hebrews 11:39).

In Acts 2:27, *"For You will not leave my soul in Hades, Nor will You allow Your Holy One to see corruption,"* and in Ephesians 4:9, "(Now this, *"He ascended"*—what does it mean but that He also first descended into the lower parts of the earth?" Jesus announced or proclaimed His resurrection from the grave, from Hades, to the believers of the Old Testament. In Matthew 27:51-53, "Then, behold, the veil of the temple was torn in two from top to bottom; and the earth quaked, and the rocks were split, [52] and the graves were opened; and many bodies of the saints who had fallen asleep were raised; [53] and coming out of the graves after His resurrection, they went into the holy city and appeared to many," those saints or believers in the Old Testament, coming out of the graves or Hades, or the comfort compartment in Hades, went into the holy city after His resurrection.

Therefore, by putting the scriptural pieces together into the whole contextual view, the comfort compartment in Abraham's bosom is no longer existent today, leaving only the torments compartment in hell. There isn't a purgatory, which is a place of purging or cleansing or waiting. If we die physically before our rapture on His coming again in Heaven, our spirit and soul will be present with the Lord immediately "For to be absent from this body is to be present with the Lord" (2 Corinthians 5:8).

In Rapture (p 188), **Partial rapture** means only mature Christians to be raptured, excluding carnal Christians, not accepted because the Bible doesn't say so.

In Millennium Kingdom (p 189), **Amillennium** (LATIN: A + Millennium)[14] means "No 1000 years." It does not mean literally in Revelation 20:4 that our Lord Jesus Christ with us will reign the earth for one thousand years, but it is symbolic or spiritual in nature at the end of the present church age. This view is not accepted because the Bible doesn't say either symbolic or spiritual meaning of 1000 years.

---

[14] See http://en.wikipedia.org/wiki/Amillennialism

2. Whole Counsel of God

(P 193-201)

Guidance

To deliver the whole counsel of God or every word, verse by verse inductive study or teaching is most effective to us. So, the Bible versions not skipped any verses (e.g., KJV, NKJV, or ASV), as the textbook, is used and other versions, sermons, or Christian books may be used as references for our faithful comprehension of God's word.

Q & A

(1) Why do I study the entire Bible?

Because God wants us to live by every word of God, neither adding nor taking away (Matthew 4:4; Hebrews 5:12-14; Acts 20:27; 2 Timothy 3:16; Deuteronomy 4:2; Revelation 22:18-19).

(2) How many books of the Bible? What is The Old Testament? What is The New Testament?

The Bible contains 66 Books, whose the Old Testament is 39 Books and the New Testament is 27 Books. The Old Testament contains 17 Historical Books, 5 Poetical Books, and 17 Prophetic Books, while the New Testament contains 4 Gospels, 1 Acts, 21 Epistles, and 1 Revelation.

(3) What is prophecy?

Prophecy is the delivered God's words in 3 ways – foretelling, forthtelling, and mutual-telling.

(4) What is a guideline for the Bible study? Do I use it today?

A guideline is suggested for the Bible study of a prayer, observation, interpretation, application, and a prayer in order.

(5) What is a context or a syntax approach?

A syntax approach is to observe and interpret the verses closed to a studied or taught verse, while a context approach is to extend from the studied or taught verse to its entire chapter, up to the book.

Supplement

In the study of **the Historical Books** (p 194), especially "I Kings, II Kings, I Chronicles, and II Chronicles," the times' order of the Kings of Israel and Judah is often questioned but archaeologically discovered times are various. A Timeline chart as a mere tool is helpful to understand the books unless it is contrary to the Word of God. Also in the study of **the Prophetic Books,** the times' order of the Prophets (early 2 prophets, 4 prophets in 5 major prophetic books, and 12 prophets in 12 minor prophetic books) in the Book is helpful because of the same reason. Here is set up the following chart as to **the Time Order of the**

Kings and the Prophets (these times are "about" or "approximate" due to the various, different, or inconsistent discovered times. Further discoveries may make clear up some inconsistent times):

Time Table of Church History[15]

931 BC	Kingdom Divided Between Judah & Israel
722 BC	Assyria conquered Israel
586 BC	Babylon conquered Judah
536 BC	Persia conquered Babylon

Time Order (#) of the Kings and the Prophets[16]

#	Israel's Kings (Reference)	Reign Period	#	Judah's Kings (reference)	Reign Period	#	Prophets (Life[17])	Reference (Bible; Kings)
1	Jeroboam (1 Ki 12:25-33)	931-910	1	Rehoboam (1 Ki 11:43)	931-913	1	Elijah (875-850)	1 Ki 15-24 Jehoshapat ; 1 Ki 16:28 Ahab
2	Nadab (1 Ki 14:20;	910-909	2	Abijam (1 Ki 14:31)	913-911	2	Elisha (850-	1 Ki 22:50

---

[15] For detail, see above, page 46.

[16] Joseph P. Free and Howard F. Vos, "Archaeology and Bible History," (Michigan; ZondervanPublishingHouse, 1950).

[17] Henry H. Halley, (ibid.).

	15:25)						800)	Jehoram
3	Baasha (1 Ki 15:16, 28)	909-886	3	Asa[18] (1 Ki 15:8)	911-870	7	Isaiah (745-695)	2 Ki 15:7 Jotham
4	Elah (1 Ki 16:6)	886-885	4	Jehoshaphat (1 Ki 15:24)	870-848	11	Jeremiah[19] (626-586)	2 Ki 23:34 Jehoiakim [Eliakim]
5	Zimri (1 Ki 16:11)	885	5	Jehoram[20] (1 Ki 22:50)	848-841			
	Tibni (1 Ki 16:21)	885-880	6	Ahaziah (2 Ki 8:24)	841			
6	Omri (1 Ki 16:16)	880-874		Athaliah[21] (2 Ki 11:1)	841-835	15	Ezekiel (592-570)	Babylon conquered Judah
7	Ahab[22] (1 Ki 16:28)	874-853	7	Joash (2 Ki 11:21)	835-796	14	Daniel (606-534)	
8	Ahaziah (1	853-	8	Amaziah (2	796-	6	Hosea	2 Ki 15:7

---

[18] Boldfaced lettered Kings are the good kings who generally obeyed the Lord.

[19] He also wrote the book of "Lamentations."

[20] Ahab's son-in-law

[21] Ahaziah's mother, Ahab's daughter (2 Ki 8:18, 26)

[22] Jezebel, his wife, and Athaliah, his daughter, who married Jehoram, the 5th Judah's King, whose father was Jehoshaphat, the 4th Judah's King who was good.

	Ki 22:40)	852		Ki 12:21)	767		(760-720)	Jotham
9	Jehoram [23] (2 Ki 1:17)	852-841	9	**Azariah** [Uzziah] (2 Ki 14:21; 2 Ch 26)	767-740	3	Joel (840-830)	2 Ki 11:21 Joash
10	Jehu (2 Ki 9:13)	841-814	10	**Jotham** (2 Ki 15:7; 2 Ch 27)	740-736	5	Amos (780-740)	2 Ki 15:7 Jotham
11	Jehoahaz (2 Ki 10:35; 13:1)	814-798	11	Ahaz (2 Ki 15:38; 2 Ch 28)	736-716	13	Obadia (586 - ?)	2 Ki 24:17 Zedekiah
12	Jehoash (2 Ki 13:9)	798-782	12	**Hezekiah** (2 Ki 16:20; 2 Ch 29)	716-687	4	Jonah (790-770)	2 Ki 14:21 Azariah [Uzziah]
13	Jeroboam II (2 Ki 14:16)	782-753	13	Manasseh (2 Ki 20:21; 2 Ch 33)	687-642	8	Micah (740-700)	2 Ki 15:38 Ahaz
14	Zechariah (2 Ki 14:29; 15:8)	753-752	14	Amon (2 Ki 21:18)	642-640	10	Nahum (630-610)	2 Ki 23:30 Jehoahaz
15	Shallum (2 Ki 15:10)	752	15	**Josiah** (2 Ki 21:24)	640-609	12	Habakuk (606-586)	2 Ki 24:6 Jehoiachin

---

[23] Jehoram, the 9th Israel's king, was killed with Ahaziah, the 6th Judah's King, by Jehu (2 Ki 9:21-27).

16	Menahem (2 Ki 15:14)	752-742	16	Jehoahaz [Shallum] [24] (2 Ki 23:30)	609	9	Zephaniah (639-608)	2 Ki 21:24 Josiah
17	Pekhiah (2 Ki 15:22)	742-740	17	Jehoiakim [Eliakim] (2 Ki 23:34)	609-597	16	Haggai (520-516)	Persia conquered Babylon: (1) return from the captivity: Joshua & Zerubbabel (536-516) (2) Temple rebuilt: Ezra (457-430) & Nehemiah (444-432)
18	Pekah (2 Ki 15:25)	740-732	18	Jeohoiachin [Jeconiah] (2 Ki 24:6; Jer 24:1)	597	16	Zechariah (520-516)	
19	Hoshea (2 Ki 15:30)	732-722	19	Zedekiah (2 Ki 24:17)	597-586	18	Malachi (450-400)	

The **prophecy** (p 194) in the 17 Prophetic Books of the Old Testament was mostly to tell the word of God to be fulfilled in the future from the

---

[24] Jehoahaz's decedents – Jehoiachin the king, his grandson, and the other three (3) kings, his sons.

time of each prophecy, i.e., fore-telling, ending in John the Baptist's in Matthew 11:13, "For all the prophets and the law prophesied until John." However, the gift of prophecy (p 61) in the New Testament means usually to tell forth the word of God, i.e., forth-telling, limited to "edification, exhortation, and comfort" (in 1 Corinthians 14:3).

In **the unit to measure** length, weight, and volume in the Bible, we need conversion to U.S. unit or Metric unit to understand how much it was. But archeologists discovered that amounts of the units were various and so the conversed amounts are "about," or "approximate." Further discoveries may make clear up some unclear amounts.

Conversion Table[25]
US Unit to Metric Unit

	US Unit		Metric Unit
Length	1 inch		2.54 centimeters (cm) (100 cm = 1 meter)
Weight	1 pound		453.59 grams (1,000 grams = 1 kilogram)
	1 ounce		28.35 grams
Volume	1 bushel = 8 gallons	Dry only	35.20 liters
	1 gallon	Liquid	3.79 liters (I liter = 1,000 cubic centimeters (cc))
		Dry	4.4 liters

---

[25] Holy Bible, New International Version, "The Holy Bible Korean and English," (Seoul, Korea: Korean Bible Society, 1995).

		Liquid	0.95 liter
1 quart = a quarter of 1 gallon (= 2 pints)		Dry	1.10 liters
1 pint = a half of 1 quart		Liquid	475 cc
		Dry	550 cc

Biblical Unit, US Unit, and Metric Unit

	Biblical Unit		US Unit	Metric Unit
Length	cubit		18 inches	45.72 cm
	Span		9 inches	22.86 cm
	Handbreadth		3 inches	7.62 cm
Weight	talent (=60 minas)		75 pounds	34.02 kg
	mina (=50 shekels)		1 ¼ pounds	566.99 g
	shekel (= 2 bekas)		2/5 ounce	11.34 g
	pim (= 2/3 shekel)		1/3 ounce	9.45 g
	beka (= 10 gerahs)		1/5 ounce	5.67 g
	Gerah		1/50 ounce	0.57 g
Volume	Liquid	bath (= 1 epha)	6 gallons	22.74 liters
		hin (=1/6 bath)	1 gallon	3.79 liters
		log (1/72 bath)	1/3 quart	0.32 liter
	Dry	cor (=homer;10 ephahs)	6 bushels	211.20 liters
		lethech (=5 ephahs)	3 bushels	105.60 liters
		ephah (10 omers)	3/5 bushel	21.12 liters
		seah (1/3 ephah)	7 quarts	7.7 liters

		omer (1/10 ephah)	2 quarts	2.2 liters
		cab (1/18 ephah)	½ pint	275 cc

Bible Maps are helpful for us to understand His word faithfully. Most the Bible Books contain Bible Maps & Places in their appendixes. We may use them to see how our Lord led people in the Bible. Also, we can use other Bible Maps & Places through an internet or a bookstore search first for a big picture and then for detail. For example, here are free the Bible maps:

http://www.ebibleteacher.com/imagehtml/otmaps.html
http://www.ebibleteacher.com/imagehtml/ntmaps.html

We should note that some places and routes discovered by archeologists are various, different, or inconsistent, showing insufficient human thoughts. Further discoveries may make clear up some unclear places and routes. So, we should wait on the Lord to reveal them, remembering "our substance is of Christ (Colossians 2:17)."

Here are references for the study of the entire Bible or for **the Whole Counsel of God:**

http://www.thewordfortoday.org/?page=C2000
http://www.calvarychapelanaheimhills.com/OnlineSermon2011.htm
http://www.calvarychapelanaheimhills.com/OnlineSermon2010.htm
http://www.calvarychapelanaheimhills.com/OnlineSermon2009.htm

The Lord's Prayer

(P 202-204)

Guidance

The Lord's Prayer as our prayer's model tells us how to pray.

Q & A

(1) What's a big picture for the Lord's prayer?

Two parts in a big picture are Worship and Petition.

(2) Can I explain the contents of my prayer?

Our prayer often begins/ends in worship throughout petitions for God, us, or others.

(3) What is the purpose of prayer? What is intercession? What is supplication?

The purpose of prayer is seeking His will in the Spirit and the Word of God. Intercession is the prayer which petitions for others. Supplication is fervent prayer.

Supplement

Worship (p 202) of our prayer simply means "to honor God," to praise God, or to glorify God. We may bring "God's characteristics" such as omnipotence, omniscience, foreknowledge, omnipresence, or creator. Thanks to the Lord may be raised. Here is an example in Acts 4:24, "So when they heard that, they raised their voice to God with one accord and said: "Lord, You *are* God, who made heaven and earth and the sea, and all that is in them.""

Fasting Prayer is a way of prayers like supplication (p 203) or fervent prayer. Under special circumstances – sorrow, affliction, repentance, protection, or a dedication – the Spirit naturally leads our broken heartily prayer deep into the fasting prayer to humble ourselves. Sorrow (e.g. "the bridegroom taken away" in Luke 5:35), affliction (e.g., "they were sick" in Psalm 35:13; "the devil cast away" in Matthew 17:18-21), repentance (e.g. "Turn to Me with all your heart" in Joel 2:12), protection ("seek from Him the right way for us" in Ezra 8:21), or a dedication (before Jesus' first dedicated ministry on the earth in Matthew 4:2; before Paul and Barnabas dedicated as missionaries in Acts 13:2-3; Anna's dedicated prayer waiting for Messiah in Luke 2:37). Fasting is only before God, not before people (Matthew 6:16). Fasting itself is not always required in Matthew 9:14, although prayer is always required in 1 Thessalonians 5:17. However, fasting naturally comes out of our broken heartily prayers as a way of a fervent prayer by the Holy Spirit.

Personal Questions

(P 205-212)

Guidance

Our answer to personal questions (1) shows what we believe and what we are given talents and (2) guides us where we are able to minister for the Kingdom of God.

Q & A

(1) Who is my leader during my life?

The Holy Spirit, not any creatures (e.g., self, a philosopher, money, glory, etc.), should be our leader during our lives.

(2) What is my compelling motive to minister?

"Love of Christ" should be my compelling motive to minister to the Lord and His sheep (2 Corinthians 5:14).

(3) Am I faithful to the Lord?

We as servants of Christ are required to be faithful (1 Corinthians 4:1-2).

(4) Am I humble?

We as Christ-like people should be humble (Philippians 2:6-7).

(5) What's controlling factor to say negative thing?

A controlling factor to say negative thing is to edify or build up the body of Christ (Galatians 2:11-23).

(6) Do I speak in the sight of Christ?

We should speak in the sight of God in Christ (2 Corinthians 2:17).

Supplement

In Galatians 6:2, "Bear one another's burdens, and so fulfill the law of Christ," we should love each other, fulfilling the greatest commandments of Agape love of God and of our neighbors, i.e. the law of Christ. **Agape love is supreme** over anything else, in 1 Corinthians 13:1-3, "Though I speak with the tongues of men and of angels, but have not love, I have become sounding brass or a clanging cymbal. ^{2} And though I have *the gift of* prophecy, and understand all mysteries and all knowledge, and though I have all faith, so that I could remove mountains, but have not love, I am nothing. ^{3} And though I bestow all my goods to feed *the poor,* and though I give my body to be burned, but have not love, it profits me nothing." So, our daily life needs **a close relationship with God in Christ** because the Agape love only comes from God, as the fruit of the Spirit of God.

Appendix 2

BYLAWS
OF
CALVARY CHAPEL OF ANAHEIM HILLS, INC.

(P 213-234)

Guidance

This kind of bylaws might guide for our church life how to serve the Lord in a local church governed by an earthly authority (a city, a county, a state, and federal government) ordained by God (Romans 13:1-2), according to the word of God.

Supplement

Any disputes in Church[26] (p 227) brought to an earthly court or earthly **litigation**, not being witnesses to Christ in the world, is discouraged in the Bible. Jesus says in Matthew 18:15-17, "Moreover (1) if your brother sins against you, go and tell him his fault between you and him alone. If he hears you, you have gained your brother. [16] But (2) if he will not hear, take with you one or two more, that *'by the mouth of two or three witnesses every word may be established.'* [17] And (3) if he refuses to hear them, tell *it* to the church. But (4) if he refuses even to hear the church, let him be to you like a heathen and a tax collector." And God

---

[26] Dispute between an earthly authority or unbelievers a believer or church, please see http://pacificjustice.org/

says through Paul in 1 Corinthians 6:6, "But brother goes to law against brother, and that before unbelievers!" Therefore, we may adopt five (5) steps according to the word of God – (1) in a local church, resolution between a wrong doer & a victim, (2) in the church, resolution with the disputers and their witnesses, (3) in the church, the church board resolves the dispute, (4) in the United States, the Christian arbitration or mediation (which applies God's word and earthly relevant law but God's word is superior to the earthly law) will resolve it. For example;

Peacemaker Ministries for Christian Conciliation
PO Box 81130, Billings, MT 59108, Tel 406-256-1583
www.peacemaker.net; http://thechurchcounsel.com/;
http://www.christian-legalaid.org/

However, if a wrong doer refuses to hear (5) we'll treat him as an unbeliever. So it is adopted in the Bylaws as "Should any disputes develop in, from, with, or to the Church, the board shall resolve them according to Matthew 18:15-17. But they not resolved shall be subject to a Christian mediation and arbitration process (e.g. peace maker ministries, Christian Legal Aid, etc.), according to 1 Corinthians 6:6, rather than an earthly Court."

Gifts designated for special purposes (p 228) is called designated offering (DO). For example, an offering is particularly given to a missionary or a poor person or a mission country. However, sometimes the DO not once is made but long time (e.g. year, years, or life time) is made. Then, DO is called as **vow, oath, or pledge**, which is an irrevocable unilateral promise. The vow is often discouraged, because we as imperfect people might not be able to keep it accordingly in Mathew 5:34-37, "But I say to you, do not swear at all: neither by heaven, for it is God's throne; ³⁵ nor by the earth, for it is His footstool; nor by Jerusalem, for it is the city of the great King. ³⁶ Nor shall you swear by your head, because you cannot make one hair white or black. ³⁷ But let your 'Yes' be 'Yes,' and your 'No,' 'No.' For whatever is more than these is from the evil one," and in James 5:12, "But above all, my brethren, do not swear, either by heaven or by earth or with any other oath. But let your "Yes" be "Yes," and *your* "No," "No," lest you fall into judgment." However, when we make a vow, we must keep it in Deuteronomy 23:21-23, "When you make a vow to the LORD your God, you shall not delay to pay it; for the LORD your God will surely require it of you, and it would be sin to you. ²² But if you abstain from vowing, it shall not be sin to you. ²³ That which has gone from your lips you shall keep and perform, for you voluntarily vowed to the LORD your God what you have promised with your mouth." In reality, the Spirit naturally leads our heart into a vow under special circumstances (e.g. baby dedication, marriage, witness testimony, or long time DO).

All compensation and reimbursement shall not exceed 50% of the all revenues at this Church (p 228). We discussed in pages 137-138 that revenue is expended in 4 ways (feeding sheep, delivering Gospel, Charity, and Ministries). So, this means that ministries' expense shall not exceed 50% of the all revenues.   This practice proves that this Church is the Lord's church in light of Matthew 16:18, "And I also say to you that you are Peter, and on this rock I will build My church, and the gates of Hades shall not prevail against it," and in John 21:15, "So when they had eaten breakfast, Jesus said to Simon Peter, "Simon, *son* of Jonah, do you love Me more than these?" He said to Him, "Yes, Lord; You know that I love You." He said to him, "Feed <u>My lambs</u>." Any churches are His church because the Lord has bought each believer with His bloodshed (1 Corinthians 6:19-20). But we often called a senior pastor's church, or a believer's church, that does not mean a church owned by either a senior pastor or a believer but a member of that church. Therefore, such a term as a human being's church should be abstained because of such possible misunderstanding unless its meaning is cleared up. Also, a pastor is sometimes called as a "reverend" in light of 1 Timothy 5:17, "Let the elders who rule well be counted worthy of <u>double honor</u>, especially <u>those who labor in the word and doctrine</u>." But since the reverend title is God's name in Psalm 111:9 (KJV), "He sent redemption unto his people: he hath commanded his covenant for ever: holy and <u>reverend is his name</u>," the **reverend** title to the pastor should be abstained.

In epilogue, we are singing the fresh song of "As The Deer[27]" from our hearts to praise our Lord at the Fountain the Bible Study members:

> "As the deer panteth for the water
> So my soul longeth after Thee
> You alone are my heart's desire
> And I long to worship Thee
>
> You alone are my strength, my shield

---

[27] Marty Nystrom, "As The Deer" (California: Maranatha Praise, Inc. 1984).

To You alone may my spirit yield
You alone are my heart's desire
And I long to worship Thee

You are my friend and
You are my brother
Even though You are a King
I love You more than
Any other
So much more than anything

You alone are my strength, my shield
To You alone may my spirit yield
You alone are my heart's desire
And I long to worship Thee

I want You more than
Gold or Silver
Only You can satisfy
You alone are the real joy-giver
And the apple of my eye

You alone are my strength, my shield
To You alone may my spirit yield
You alone are my heart's desire
And I long to worship Thee "

Amen

Dr Wayne Kim is a Pastor and Teacher of Calvary Chapel Anaheim Hills in Anaheim Hills, California. He was born in spirit of Buddhism, mixed with Confucianism, and grew up in the fear of death until youth. After becoming a born again Christian, he faced turmoil of denominations, evolutionism, postmodernism, the word of faith, prosperity gospel, and other thoughts, etc, resulting in his emptiness and his thirst for truth. While he was a college teacher and Sunday School the Bible teacher, his deeper thirst for the Word of God led him to go to study theology and the Bible at the School of Ministry at Calvary Chapel Costa Mesa, where he has been taught, influenced, and mentored by Pastors Carl Westurlund, Chuck Smith, and Duke Kim. Chuck impacted on him to have an answer his life time thirst to be filled in the balance between the teaching of the Whole Counsel of God and an open heart to the work of the Holy Spirit. After being called a pastor, he has met people and preached Gospel and taught the Bible, thinking of every thought how to be subject to the knowledge of God. Throughout his taught thoughts and experiences, how our Lord is leading our life in the Whole Counsel of God is spiritually, biblically, empirically, and practically discussed in a depth in "Guidance, Q & A, or Supplement to The Spirit Led^{TM} Life in the Whole Counsel of God." To anyone who wants to be the Spirit Led Life, this The Spirit Led^{TM} Life book would be helpful and profitable to study or teach every word of the Bible with that Guidance, Q & A, or Supplement book in depth.

"Go therefore and make disciples of all the nations…" (Matthew 28:19a)

- **Contact or free will Offering for World DISCIPLE Mission:** CCAH, PO Box 27693, Anaheim Hills, CA 92809, USA (714) 797-0454 www.CalvaryChapelAnaheimHills.com
- **Source of the Cover Photo:** www.sxc.hu
- **Order of the Books:** www.Amazon.com